Sandy Kreamer

A Menu
of
Memories

Copyright © 1998 by Sandra Kreamer

ISBN 0-9654086-1-2

Library of Congress Catalog Number: 97-94568

Printed in the United States of America.

J I H G F E D C B A

This book is dedicated to my grandchildren and great grandchildren with the purpose of acquainting them to their family they can no longer touch, see or feel. Family members gone before them. These people have helped you become what you are.

With much love, I introduce you to all the family I can give you in hopes of a better understanding of your roots and the importance of continuing our family tree of life.

I pray you, my grandchildren and great grandchildren, are strong in mind and body. I may not be here to kiss and hug you, but you will always be forever in my heart.

"Family is one of the chief abodes of soul."

"Family is the next of which soul is born,
nurtured and released into life."

"Family is to the individual what the
origins of human life are to race."

"A piece of sky and a chunk of earth lie
lodged into the heart of every human being."

from *Care of the Soul*
by Thomas Moore

Table of Contents

What's Behind
A Menu of Memories

I felt this book needed to be written, not only to bring to life my family's history, but to view the kaleidoscope of its colorful characters. This book is to be used as a guide and window, helping you and those who come after you on your travels in life. It will give future generations the knowledge of their beginnings, who and where they came from. These seeds are all your family's souls before you.

This book is written not only for my children, but for my children's children, and for generations thereafter, as long as this lineage continues. It is filled with pictures and memories of past generations, along with recipes that came with them.

I have done research in the National Archives in Washington, DC to find out more about our family origins. Some of the names I discovered may not hold much meaning for you, so I have found as many pictures as I could. These photographs will help the people become more alive as you read about them and learn what they brought to your life before you were born.

I hope you will enjoy reading and using this book as much as I have enjoyed writing it.

Love,

Sandy

One

Seeds of
Our Family

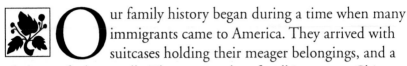**O**ur family history began during a time when many immigrants came to America. They arrived with suitcases holding their meager belongings, and a plethora of tales to tell. There were tales of walking across China to get to the ocean and sailing for America, as one of my uncles did. Tales of fighting against the Czar in the Russian underground. Tales of having families torn apart by wars. Tales of two brothers killing themselves for the rest of the family's safety.

Many relatives became family heroes in these struggles to survive and live in a new, better way, in a new, better land.

The beginnings of our family's story were difficult to find. There are no written records of the births of our ancestors in Europe until 1865. This was deliberate. Because throughout history Jews had been persecuted, tortured, and killed, Jewish births were not recorded in the hope of protecting children's lives. That year, 1865, was the year my great-grandfather, Moritz Monchane, was born in Cairo, Egypt.

My great-grandmother's mother, Yenta, is our only ancestor before Moritz and his wife Rebecca that any of us ever heard about. She had a general store in Romania called Zalaman's, where she filled medical prescriptions. Unfortunately, no one has any memories or stories about her to pass on.

My great-grandfather Moritz became known to me through a photo of him and his wife, my great grandmother Rebecca. They were my father's grandparents, and my grandmother Tina's parents. I began making as many inquiries about them as I could, talking to older family relatives and trying to piece the stories together. In these stories—many of which follow in this book—people suddenly began to come alive to me.

Moritz and Rebecca in the U.S. in front of their home in the late 30s

Moritz Monchane

Moritz was a short, strong and very handsome man. In his younger days, he was a chef aboard ships that sailed the Mediterranean Sea. (I like to think that my own cooking expertise can be traced back to Moritz.)

While working aboard ship on one of his journeys, Moritz developed a terrible pain in his stomach. It was diagnosed as appendicitis, and nothing could be done until the ship docked. But by the time he reached shore, the infection had run throughout his body and gangrene had developed in his leg. He survived, but had to have his leg amputated. He wore a wooden leg from then on.

Moritz met young Rebecca Segal when his ship docked in Bucharest, Romania for supplies and fell madly in love with her. He never returned to the ship. Moritz married her in Bucharest, and together they began their family. They had nine children—seven girls and two boys—before entertaining the idea of coming to America.

Moritz left his home in Romania on April 16, 1910, at age 45, and never looked back. He came across the ocean aboard the SS George Washington, sailing out of Bremen, Germany. He brought with him one of his nine children, leaving the rest in the old country with Rebecca. She and the others would join them after Moritz had earned enough money for their safe passage to America.

He and his children arrived in this country at the port outside New York City called Ellis Island. Their entrance into the United States is shown on a ship's documents obtained from the National Archives. These papers begin the written record for this side of our family in America. (The ship's manifest states that Moritz was born in Bucharest, but this is not true.)

Upon his arrival in America, Moritz and his child traveled directly to Minneapolis. Coming to America—with a new language, new surroundings, and a child to raise—must have been very difficult, not to mention frightening.

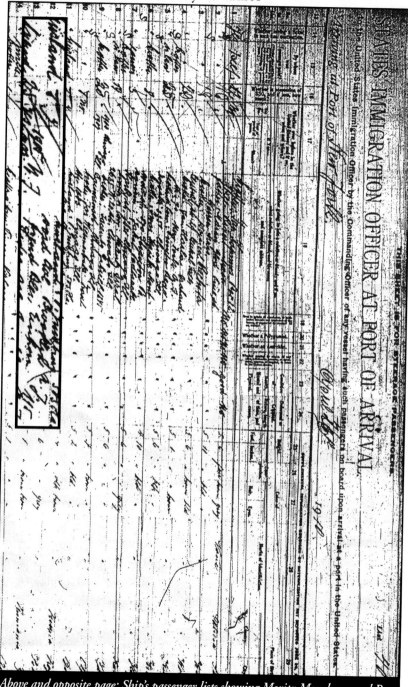

Above and opposite page: Ship's passenger lists showing Moritz Monchane and Rose, one of his daughyer's, leaving Europe and arriving in America.

A brilliant and very learned man, Moritz was entirely self-taught. He spoke seven languages and was completely fluent in French. He loved to laugh, but he could also be a very harsh man when he felt he was being ignored or not listened to. He was small in stature, but big in his demands on himself and his family. He demanded total, unconditional respect from his wife and children.

After he landed in America and found work, it took Moritz only a year to save enough money to have his family in Romania join him. Unfortunately, the money he sent them was quickly stolen. Thus, Rebecca and her other children had to make the long voyage across the ocean in steerage, along with all the cargo, rather than in the safety and comfort Moritz had planned for them. They left from Antwerp, Belgium in 1911.

The voyage was a nightmare. During the trip, the youngest of the children, Fanny, a little over one-year old, developed a raging fever, which caused her convulsions. There was no doctor aboard the ship, leaving the captain to attend any illness. He told my great-grandmother that Fanny should be thrown overboard because no one knew what had caused her illness, and it might be contagious. He added that he thought the fever and convulsions would kill her anyway.

Rebecca refused, and Fanny did not die. She did, however, become brain damaged and retarded for the rest of her life. But the family cared for her until her death in her seventies.

The rest of the Monchanes arrived healthy. They reunited and set up housekeeping in north Minneapolis.

Moritz worked as a baker on Washington Avenue in Minneapolis, at a restaurant called Sherman's, from 1921 until the late 1930s, when he retired. His favorite task was making raisin bread on Fridays. This bread was challah and he baked it for the Sabbath. He would always take home a couple of loaves for his family, and every Saturday night they would enjoy bread made by the best baker in the family. As Moritz's children grew up and began marrying, they would regularly bring their spouses and children to Zayda's house on Saturday night for raisin bread.

Moritz loved being fully in charge of his family. He enjoyed entertaining friends as well, and always took great pride in his cooking, his presentation of food, and his table settings. (He was very knowledgeable about proper etiquette.) After his retirement, he continued to bake in his home and still expected to receive visits and adoration from his family on bread-baking days.

One of the few memories I have of Moritz is when I was three years old. I would crawl under the large family table during holiday dinners, and knock on his wooden leg to hear its hollow sound and touch its hardness. He never felt me doing it, but I remember the noise of my little fist upon that hollow wood, slightly muffled by his trousers.

Moritz died peacefully in the home of one of his grandchildren, my cousin Dorothy—one of his eldest daughter's children, with whom he lived until his death in 1946 at the age of 81. He left behind nine children and at least 15 grandchildren.

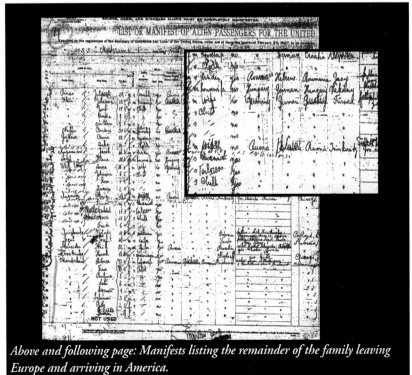

Above and following page: Manifests listing the remainder of the family leaving Europe and arriving in America.

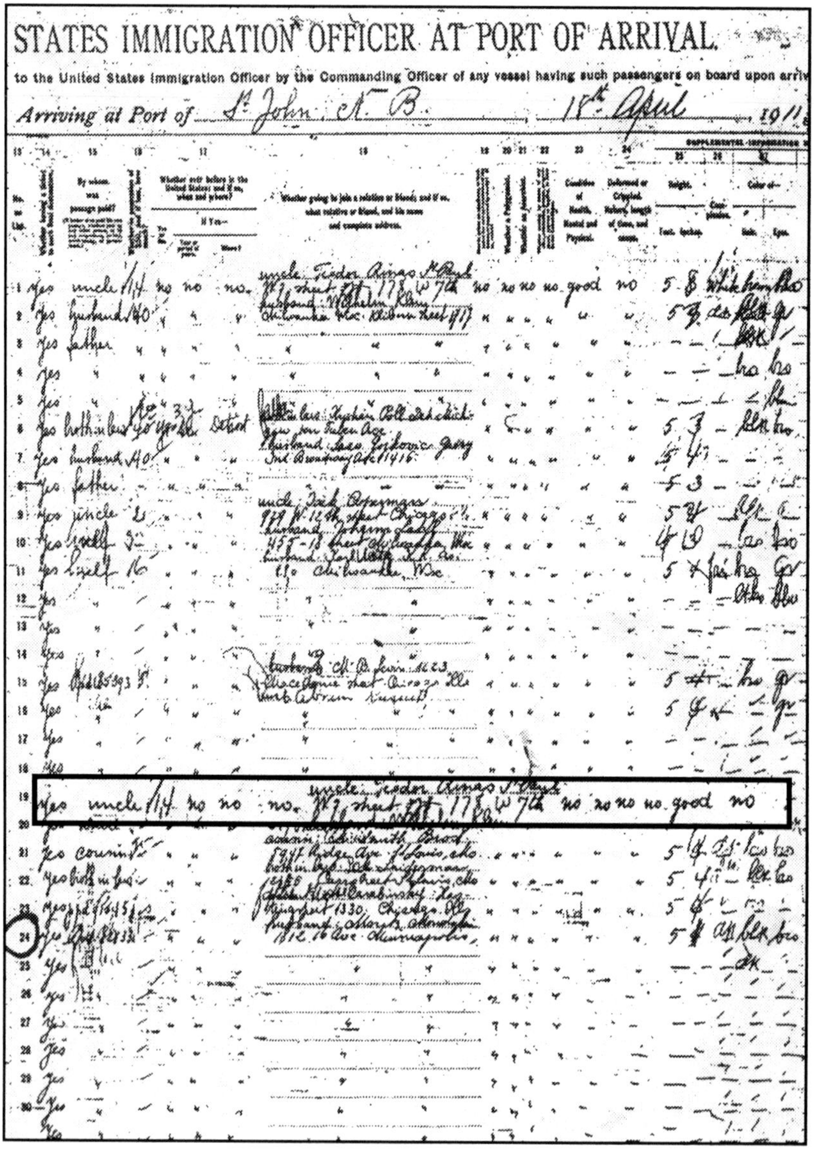
STATES IMMIGRATION OFFICER AT PORT OF ARRIVAL.

to the United States Immigration Officer by the Commanding Officer of any vessel having such passengers on board upon arriv

Arriving at Port of St. John N. B. 18th April 1911

Rebecca Monchane

Rebecca was a soft, quiet woman, much larger in stature than my great-grandfather. She loved every one of her nine children, doing her best to raise and support them until the end of her life.

She was only 53 years old when she passed away from a stroke—the result of high blood pressure. At that point only a few of their children were married, so from then on—with the help of the older siblings—Moritz raised the younger children. He never remarried, and for the rest of his life was not the same man.

Everyone who knew Rebecca remembered her with great affection. As I write this section in early 1997, only one of her children is still alive; my Aunt Jessie, now in her 89th year and still very active. Jessie was taught by her father to speak fluent French. He also made her take piano lessons as a child, and she still plays beautifully at 89, with her gnarled fingers and beautifully manicured fingernails polished bright red. Aunt Jessie spent Rosh Hashana with us a few years ago and brought honey cake. This recipe came from her mom—my children's great-great-grandmother.

The descendants of Rebecca and Moritz now live all across the United States, but the vast majority still reside in the suburbs of Minneapolis. We are now on the fourth generation of family members in America, each with their own stories. I have not kept track of what each one is doing, but do see them occasionally at B'nai Emet a synagogue in St. Louis Park—where they have been members all these generations. (For our family, B'nai Emet has been a gathering place in good times and bad, and it appears to still be the thread that holds our family together.)

With the exception of Fanny, all nine of Moritz and Rebecca's children married and had children, and as adults all nine lived within a few blocks of each other in Minneapolis. As a result, I grew up with a very large family of cousins, aunts, and uncles, all living within walking distance of my home.

The generations have changed, but in some ways the faces have not. We all continue to resemble the Monchanes in one way or another. That link will always be there.

Moritz and Rebecca's children. Standing, left to right: Sophie, Selma, Phil, Izzie, Tina, Lilly, Mary, Irving, Jerry (Sophie's son). Kneeling, left to right: Bill, Sol, and Barbara. Not shown: Fannie and Jessi.

Tina Kreamer-"Grandma Tina"

Grandma Tina

The next generation began with my Grandma Tina, one of Moritz and Rebecca's seven girls. She was a diminutive lady whom I remember fondly. She was sixteen when she arrived in America with her mother, and, as far as I know, had a conventional family life until her mother's death. She remained close to her father and siblings throughout her life.

Grandma Tina played a significant role in my life. As her first grandchild, and the first girl in my grandmother's life (she had no daughters), I became her world. She'd walk to our house with halvah in her pocket for me when I was ill. She would sit by my bed for hours when I was sick, soothing and comforting me with her presence as well as the halvah.

My grandparents lived across the alley from us, and their home became my haven. Whenever I ran away from home, everyone knew to look for me there.

My grandma and I were always together. Often we'd bake poppyseed cookies, using a glass to cut out the shapes. I'd wear a kitchen towel as an apron, and she'd wear her long yellow-flowered apron tied at the waist. In the summer, we'd eat ice cream together on her steps while watching people get off the streetcar two houses down. (My grandparents lived at the end of the streetcar line on Sheridan Avenue in North Minneapolis. After letting off the last of his riders, the conductor would have to get out and turn the car around, making sure it was still attached to the crisscrossing electric wires overhead.)

While watching the world go by, Grandma Tina would tell me stories about her life in Europe as a young child. The stories were filled with gypsies stealing children who weren't theirs, then selling them as workers, or to people who wanted children but couldn't have their own.

I would often sit at the desk in my grandparents' sunroom, pretending to be a writer or just dreaming. This room was in the front of their house, facing the street. I liked it there because I could easily spy on the neighbors without being seen as they went about their daily tasks.

Every summer I helped my grandfather Isadore—I called him Papa—water his tomatoes. I stole apples and plums off their trees. I listened to their windup clock ticking away the seconds in their kitchen when I slept in their home.

Sometimes very early on Sunday mornings, before my parents woke, I would wake my younger sister Bitsy. Half-conscious, I would help her dress while my parents slept soundly down the hall. Then, using flashlights so as not to wake anyone, we would walk down the dark, silent hall, put on our coats and boots, and slip outside. Our plan was to walk to my grandparents' house and surprise them and, of course, get invited for breakfast.

They lived only a few blocks away, but the trip seemed like miles. We would become tremendously hungry and dream of all the good food Grandma would make for us. In the winter, to stay warm while walking in the deepest snow, I would pretend I was in a desert, walking on hot sand, and if I wasn't fast enough, I would burn my bare feet.

We would always try to surprise Grandma and Grandpa, but somehow they always knew when we were on our way. When we finally reached their house, Grandma would be dressed and waiting for us, with big cups of hot milk coffee in hand. Hugs, kisses, and smiles would follow.

My Grandma Tina was always shy about her body. She would get dressed and undressed in her huge bedroom closet. In it hung a number of purses, where she saved all her extra money for us for candy or ice cream. I never could understand why she was that shy. Finally, when I was older, I was told she had had breast cancer, and a breast had been removed. From then on she felt ashamed of her body, believing the cancer and mastectomy to be punishments from God. (She had learned this superstition about abnormalities as a child in Romania and still felt she had to hide her body.)

I remember many wonderful smells swirling around the stove in my grandma's kitchen. It was a large, square room with a wonderful chrome and metal table with a drawer under its ceramic top for her silverware. I spent many hours standing on a chair next to her, playing with cookie dough and watching the curtains above us sway with the breeze that glided in through the open windows. Often we would sit at the table, eating plums from her trees or peeling the skin off the green apples we found on the ground to make delicious pies.

In winter her kitchen windows were always steamed up from her cooking pot full of chicken soup. It was always delicious, and made with only kosher chickens. She would buy the chicken whole, then clean it out and cut it up to fit the pot. The best part was the eggs that were sometimes still inside the chicken.

Grandma Tina would carefully remove these and boil them in the soup. To my sister Bitsy and me, this was the most delicious part of the soup-a special treat. We would always look for these eggs and sometimes fight over them.

Romanians had a reputation for making wonderful cornmeal mush, referred to as mamalaga. My dad and uncles remember eating this gruel, and my father still loves it, but I don't ever remember seeing or eating it. I've written the recipe for it at the end of this book along with the recipe for Grandma Tina's wonderful poppy-seed cookies.

The eggplant Grandma Tina made was and still is the best I have ever had. I would watch her make it on the extra stove in the basement of their home. She would cook it directly on top of the gas burners which, as far as I know, was the only way she ever cooked eggplant. The burnt skin of the vegetable created a wonder-ful smell, hinting at the treat we were about to be served. (I never saw her use that stove for anything else, though her husband used it now and then to make beer and wine.) To this day, the only way I know to cook eggplant is the way she showed me. If you don't have a gas stove, you may have to do some serious improvising!

I have wonderful memories of Grandma Tina and the important place she had in my life. I carry her with me wherever I am. She is my soul. My youngest daughter, Tara, is named for her.

Stephen, my first born, knew Tina when he was very young. His only memories of her are when I would take him to visit her. He would head straight into her kitchen and look in her oven. (She kept all her treats there because her apartment was so small.) I am sorry she did not live long enough to know my children today. She would be terribly proud of all three.

The legacy Grandma Tina left will continue. I hope my grandchildren will remember me with the same warmth and love I still carry for her.

Her house still stands in north Minneapolis. The walls in each room are bathed in memories of our family's laughter, joys, and Jewish holidays spent with all my aunts, uncles and cousins—eating and laughing, eating and arguing, eating and kissing, eating and crying.

My grandparents lived in this house until my grandfather's death in 1960, when he was 72. Grandma Tina sold the house a few years later to a preacher and his family (who are still living in it). She moved into an apartment, where she lived until she died of a stroke in 1968.

Isadore Kreamer- "Papa"

My grandfather, Isadore Kreamer, was born in Lithuania. He had a brother and several sisters (nobody knows exactly how many). His mother died shortly after he was born. His father Jacob was a cabinet-maker who traveled from town to town. Finding himself with a large family and no mother to care for them while he was making a

Grandma and Papa (Isadore)

living, Jacob quickly remarried, leaving the children to be raised by their stepmother.

My grandfather, who was then a small boy, would not accept this other woman. He did not want anyone taking his mother's place. Consequently, Isadore often ran away from home in search of his father when he was out of town. When he would find him in another village, the two would stay together until the job was done, then return home. At other times Isadore would hide in the woods surrounding his small town, and his friends would bring food to him in his hiding place.

Isadore studied at the Yeshiva for a time, but because of his frequent disappearances, at the age of seven he was removed and sent away from home to apprentice with a tailor. He lived with the tailor's family while learning the trade. He worked for his room and board, receiving no other pay.

Life was very hard for him, and his living conditions were poor. He slept in a cot in the kitchen, and sometimes on top of the stove during the harsh Lithuanian winters. (He had a scar on his forehead from a fall he took one night while sleeping on top of the stove. He carried this scar as a reminder of the old country for the rest of his life.)

Isadore came to the United States from Lithuania at age 16. His sister Ann, who was already here, served as his sponsor. He arrived in New York and stayed there for one year, living with her. Then he moved to Minneapolis to live with a family named Segal. No one I have talked to knows who these people were, or if there are any living descendants.

At 17 Isadore borrowed money from the Jewish Agency of Minneapolis, bought himself a horse and wagon, and began to peddle merchandise in and around Mankato, Minnesota. He did this until 1916.

Isadore had cousins living in northern Minnesota during the summer, in what is now known as the Boundary Waters. It sounded like just the place he would love after living in the woods in Europe, so at age 18 he moved to Virginia, Minnesota. In the summer he would hunt and fish, and in the winter he worked in his cousins' place of business, Borgin's Clothing and General Store, in the small town of Ely. (People today from the Iron Range still remember this store and its owners.)

On a return trip from Ely to Minneapolis he met his future wife Tina. They married shortly afterward on February 24, 1917, and my father Edward—the first of their three sons—was born nine months later on November 26, 1918.

After Edward's birth, Isadore and Tina went back to Virginia, Minnesota. Papa wanted to be back in the great outdoors. But they lasted there only about a year; Tina became very homesick for Minneapolis and the rest of her family. She forced Papa to pack up and move back down to Minneapolis, where they would continue raising their family among relatives and familiar surroundings.

In Minneapolis they had two more sons, Jack in 1920 and Arnold in 1926. With three sons to raise, my grandpa felt they needed a home of their own. He found a piece of property at 1325 Sheridan Ave. North and built a duplex. The Kreamers lived downstairs and their renters upstairs. The extra income they received as landlords helped them Through the difficult times they knew would occasionally arrive. I remember that house with nothing but fond memories. I loved to sit halfway up the back stairs, hiding from everyone and eating picked fruit. On hot summer days I would nap with my grandma in her bed.

Papa was a quiet, hardworking man who loved me very much. I could feel his love for me emanate from his smile whenever he looked at me. He didn't kiss or hug much, but his warmth and intelligence flowed from every pore in his body.

It has been said that Papa had been married before meeting my grandmother, but no one knows anything about any other woman or any other children-or even if the story is true.

When I was 15 years old, Papa was taken to Mt. Sinai hospital. He died of an ulcerated colon and its complications while holding my hand.

Tina and Isadore's wedding picture—February 24, 1917

Home the Kreamers built in 1921 on 1325 Sheridan Avenue

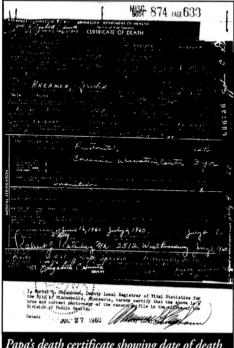

Papa's death certificate showing date of death as July 2, 1960

Sarah and Sam Starekow
- My Grandparents

My grandparents on my mother's side were both born in the same shtetl, or small village, in Russia; Sam in 1889, his future wife Sarah Wodlinger in 1891.

Sam and Sarah were first cousins. At the time, it was not unusual for cousins to marry each other; many people never left their villages, leaving them with few marriage options.

Sarah Wodlinger with Sam in Europe before they came to America to wed and make their home

Sam's father was Israel Starekow. I was unable to find any information about his mother except that she died at a young age. There is no record of her name anywhere. Sam had four brothers; unfortunately, nothing is known about any of them either.

I do know a few things about Sarah's family. She was the youngest of three children. The only names I could find in the written records are of Sarah's father, Moshe David, and one brother, Pesse. There are no other records of her family before her.

Sarah's mother died young, leaving Sarah to care for her brothers while in Russia. She became a seamstress to earn money for the family. (Sarah continued sewing for others until her death.)

The only story I was told about her family's life in Russia was the loss of two brothers during the reign of Czar Nicholas and Czarina Alexandra. Her two younger brothers were in the underground, fighting to topple Nicholas and Alexandra from power. They fought under assumed names because if the government caught them and discovered who they were, their family would be killed. (They used the names and identity papers of two soldiers who had died.) At one point, when their real identities were about to be discovered, they felt they had to kill themselves to save their family. One brother shot the other, then himself.

Sarah and Sam emigrated to America together but did not marry until after they arrived. Sara's remaining brother, came to America a year earlier.

Sarah and Sam settled in Philadelphia, where their first child, Milton, was born in 1914. But they dreamed of having lots of space and of raising their children outside the ghettos of the big city.

Sarah's brother married, and his family pioneered their way to the Dakotas. He wrote to Sarah and Sam about its open spaces, and they decided to join him on the prairie.

Soon after they arrived in Mott, North Dakota, Sam bought the creamery which served the farmers in

Sarah Wodlinger Starekow's brothers in Russia during years of fighting against the Czar in the underground before their death by their own hands

22

and around the community. Mott was a small town with a total Jewish population of three families. Indians sat, draped in blankets, on the steps of the shops. Everyone else in town was of German descent. (Mott had been settled by German farmers, and Jews were not exactly welcomed.)

This must have been very hard for Sarah and Sam. They had come to America to escape the pogroms in Russia—attacks upon Jewish settlements by men on horseback who would ride through town, hurting people and destroying their property. Now that they were here, supposedly safe, they experienced some of the same fear. Still, they stayed in Mott and raised their three children.

My grandmother Sarah tried to keep Judaism in their home, which was above the creamery. She spoke hardly any English, speaking Yiddish to Sam and the few Jewish people living in the town. She was very lonely, keeping mostly to herself.

My mother remembers her always cooking or cleaning, devoting her entire life to their care. She made all their butter and all their clothes and, when necessary, would also help in the creamery.

Creamery in Mott, North Dakota. Grandpa Sam is standing on the right.

Grandma Sarah in front of the creamery

My grandparents had two more children after arriving in Mott. Hattie was next, born December 15, 1917 and Rose, my mother's last, was born on July 13, 1920.

Their childhoods were very different from those of Jews raised in the city. They grew up with American Indians and German farmers. They had to travel to Fargo to go to the synagogue for holiday worship, and my uncle Milton had his bar mitzvah in the Mott Hotel, with a surrogate rabbi presiding.

At that time, none of the towns in North Dakota had their own rabbis and synagogues. When I was young, my uncle Milt (Sarah and Sam's son) told me about a cantor and rabbi who would travel to the various small towns on horseback to perform weddings, briss-

Sarah and Sam Starekow in car; Rose in car, Hatti and Milt on running board; neighbor's car; picture taken to be sent back to East Coast family to show them they became successful; although Sam never learned to drive. Circa 1920.

Grandpa Sam

es, and other services for Jewish families.

Grandpa Sam helped build the Jewish community and its synagogue in Fargo. He paid for the cornerstone of the synagogue, and his name was engraved deep into its surface. It can still be easily read and will remain as long as the building stands. The building is no longer a synagogue, however, and is now used as a community center.

Life was hard for Grandma Sarah in Mott. She gave birth to her children at home with a midwife and raised them as Jews as best she could. It wasn't easy trying to keep a kosher home on the prairie, trying not to be looked upon as an outsider, and trying to belong. In addition, my grandfather worked long hours, leaving Sarah the task of raising their three children— all without speaking English.

My mom developed whooping cough, and sometimes she coughed until she almost stopped breathing. My mother vividly remembers sitting next to her mom at her sewing machine, coughing and watching her work. (At that time there was no cure except to let the illness run its course.) The illness left her with weak lungs and tuberculosis near the end of her life.

The Depression did not have as large an impact on rural and small-town families as it did on city-dwellers. Cows still needed milking, and the farmers still brought their milk to the creameries in town, from which it was shipped to the dairies in larger towns to sell. The farmers did have problems toward the end of the

Sam and Sarah Starekow with their children: Milton, Rose, and Hatti. Circa 1924.

Depression, however, and at that time my grandparents decided to add a small grocery store to the creamery for extra income.

Sam died in 1936 at age 47. His body was discovered in the Missouri River in Mott, North Dakota, by kids out for an afternoon swim. It remains a mystery whether he had a fatal stroke while sitting on the dam and then fell in, or whether the stroke caused him to fall but didn't kill him, and he died by drowning. Their daughter Rose—my mother—was only sixteen at the time.

For a year or so afterward, my grandma tried to run the store by herself. During that year they traveled to larger towns on Jewish holidays, hoping to find a synagogue and a rabbi so they could be with more Jewish people and not feel so alone. But doing everything by herself soon became too difficult. Partly at her son Milton's insistence, the family sold the store, the creamery, and all they had, and Sarah and her two daughters left Mott. (Milton had already left and was attending medical school in Chicago.) The family moved to Minneapolis, where Sarah knew people and where she and her daughters could be among Jewish families.

Sam Starekows citizenship naturalization proof on February 15, 1921.

Cornerstone in one of the first synagogues in Bismark North Dakota—built with my grandfather's help.

Grandma Sarah and Papa Ben soon after their marriage in 1944.

During the first year of my life, Grandma Sarah remarried. Her new husband was Ben Cohen, a widower who owned a small neighborhood grocery store in Minneapolis. All of us called her new husband Papa Ben.

Her life was reminiscent of her previous marriage, except that instead of living above a creamery, they lived in a home attached to Papa Ben's store. They lived and worked only a few blocks from where we lived in the Projects, which made it easy to visit them.

Whenever we would visit my grandparents, I would love peeking into the store through the curtained window on the door leading to the kitchen. I would always get scolded for this, for it didn't look good to customers to see me spying on them. But it wasn't just the customers I was looking at. I just enjoyed watching Papa Ben, sitting there with his legs crossed, a dark gray wool cardigan over his slumped shoulders. He would have a serious look in his droopy eyes and a hand-rolled cigarette always in his mouth.

Sometimes Papa Ben would let me come in the store and stay behind the counter with him. The old wooden floor was always cold, and it squeaked when Papa Ben walked on it with his heavy, shiny, black shoes. The candy in the glass cases was always calling me to grab some without being noticed-which I sometimes did. I would feel big and proud behind the food cases. This was my grandpa's own store-his and his alone! How important he was! And being his granddaughter made me feel equally important.

During Jewish holidays, we always gathered for dinner with my many cousins around Grandma Sarah's beautifully laden dinner table. Her best china and silver always glistened, and her food was always delicious. My dad especially loved her beet borscht and her chicken soup, but I remember best her hamantaschen. I have never seen or tasted hamantaschen like them anywhere else. She would make regular poppy seed filling, but then she would take two arrow-root cookies-the kind you give to babies-put an inch of poppyseed filling between them, and make them into a very thick sandwich.

On Passover, we would have to sit silently at the table while Papa Ben went through the seder book only in Hebrew. He would recline on his pillow, as one should do during this holiday. He was very religious and had to be respected, or we would be sent from the table. With starved and growling stomachs, we did not move a muscle while he read the whole seder book in Hebrew. Our reward was a delicious meal.

For me, the highlights of the seder meal were chopped liver and homemade gefilte fish with strong horseradish. My grandmother always made her gefilte fish from scratch; it never came from a jar.

Papa Ben, Grandma Sarah, and cousins. Grandma's only surviving brother Pesse with his only daughter Ethle and her son sitting in front; Pesse's wife on his right.

Passover was always meaningful for us. Grandma Sarah and Papa Ben would scour their home from top to bottom before changing dishes. Our parents would buy us new spring clothes to wear to the Seder. By the time we arrived for dinner, we were always excited and exhausted.

I loved this time of the year. I knew winter was almost gone whenever Passover began. The smell of hard-boiled eggs would be in the air. Sometimes too, there would be the smell of Grandma Sarah's compote—a mixture of prunes, apricots, raisins and apples—simmering on the stove. It always made their home smell sweet. My grandparents ate this all year through, not just on holidays. When I was small I never understood why, but now I do.

I hope you will try making an entire Passover meal from scratch at least once yourself. Then you will understand the difficulty of cooking without modern conveniences. It was quite time-consuming without microwaves or double ovens.

Every Sunday afternoon, my grandparents would be all dressed up, waiting on the bench outside their house for our family to pick them up for a ride into the country. They had no car, and the rest of the week they stayed only in their house and neighborhood.

I was totally bored on those rides. We took the same route almost every Sunday. They spoke only Yiddish to each other, and I could never interrupt to ask what they were saying because that was considered rude. I would stare out the window blankly.

In the summer we would stop for an ice cream cone, but nothing more. Keeping kosher meant not being able to eat anywhere other than in a Jewish home, since at that time Minnesota had no kosher restaurants. But somehow, ice cream was considered all right to eat outside the house.

My grandma was a beautiful seamstress, and during the week she occupied her time by sewing. She made me beautiful dresses, although I hated standing on top of her kitchen table while she measured and pinned the hem of an unfinished garment. I was always afraid I would get my skin pinned to the bottom of the dress.

Even though she didn't understand much English, my grandma wanted to share something American with me, so one day she took me to the movies, and then to Bridgeman's for a sundae after the show. The problem was that she couldn't read the marquee at the theater, and she took me to the wrong movie. It was a horror movie, and I spent the entire time hiding my head in her lap. She felt awful about it, but the turtle sundae I ate afterward made up for the movie. Still, she was so embarrassed that she never took me again.

Since my grandmother Sarah never learned to speak English well, it was difficult for me to understand her—and for her to understand me. I did not have the same relationship with her that I had with my other grandma, but I loved her dearly and knew she loved me. I could feel her sadness in her very quiet demeanor as she led her life in Minneapolis as a parent and grandparent.

As a young girl, I would sometimes travel with her by train to visit my cousins, who lived in Thief River Falls, a small town in northwestern Minnesota. It was a ten-hour train ride, always overnight, and we would have a sleeping compartment. My grandma would inevitably lose her false teeth, either under the berth or in the self-contained bathroom. There would always be a rush to find them in the morning when it was time to get off the train.

I have a sad memory of the last Passover we spent with her. She was very ill with painful liver cancer and was in a hospital bed that we set up in her living room. That night she wanted no pain medication, so she could be awake to share a final Passover with her family. A trapeze bar over her head helped her when she needed to sit up or turn painfully to see us.

This once overweight, beautiful woman with long silver-gray hair was then 75 pounds and in great pain. She had a desperate need to be surrounded by her family, and now we were there with her. I went over to kiss her, feeling my own unspoken fear of death.

I saw behind those suffering eyes the great strength she once had. I never once heard her moan or cry out in pain.

The smell of death in my grandmother's house that last Passover overshadowed anything my family tried to do for her. When I looked over to her, I saw nothing but the pain she silently bore written on her face.

Meanwhile, my mother, her sister and brother, and their families went on as if all was normal. I watched as they gave my grandmother the first spoonful of chicken soup to taste, to see if it was good enough to serve us. I doubt if she could even taste it, but she nodded, and only then were the bowls filled and passed out to us.

When dinner was finished, the only place I could go to get away from this scene of death was my grandparents' bedroom. It was filled with the smell of her, the way I remembered her. The smell came from her perfume bottles, which as a child I would frequently open and sniff, filling the room with her familiar scents.

A few weeks later in 1956, my grandmother's strength finally gave out and she died quietly—where and how she wanted to, in her home in Minneapolis. Papa Ben, her second husband, was by her side. So were my mom and her sister, both of whom took care of her and were with her as she died. I was twelve at the time.

My mother and I both wish we had known her better.

From that point on, Jewish holidays were not quite the same. As for my Papa Ben, I did not see him much after that. I believe he moved to California to live with his son from his first marriage and his daughter-in-law. I thought of him often, but I never heard anything from or about him until I got married-months after he had passed away. Then, in the mail, came a beautiful bible sent to me from his family. It was a shock to me when I saw his name written on the card that accompanied this gift.

I still prize this bible, although a few dogs have chewed on it while teething as puppies. It is the only tangible proof of his existence in my life. I hold it and read its worn pages with great love and wonderful memories.

Grandma Sarah's death certificate

Edward Kreamer - My Father

My father, Ed Kreamer at 6 months old

Edward, the first child of Isadore and Tina Kreamer, was born on November 26, 1917, in Minneapolis, while Isadore was still in Virginia, Minnesota.

My dad's birth was not uneventful. My grandmother was a small woman, about 4'10" tall, and my father weighed almost twelve pounds at birth. The doctor had to pull him out by his arm and shoulder, causing all the nerves and muscles in them to tear. They never healed, and this defect has been with him throughout his life. He has never had much use of his arm, and on some days it causes him great pain.

But my sisters and I never really noticed it. He would play baseball with me and drive me where I needed to go, and the unbelievable strength in his other arm was enough to compensate. For my dad, one arm could do the job of two. (He is now 80, and his good arm is still as strong as it was when he was in his thirties.)

My dad loved to tell us stories about when he was young. One of his earliest recollections is from when he was three years old. Each day his mother would give him a penny, which he would take to a neighbor woman who raised chickens in her back yard. He would present her with the penny, and in turn she would give him an egg. He would walk carefully home with it, and his mother would cook it for him.

Isadore and Tina Kreamer; left to right: Ed, Arnold and Jack in 1928

My dad still vividly remembers the horses and carts that filled the streets. My dad's great uncle by marriage, Chaim Nacht, was a junkman, and he would travel through the alleys with his horse and wagon. Using a magnet, he would rummage through people's yards and trash, scavenging for metal to sell to scrap dealers.

The Nachts' house stood on Bryant Avenue North between 4th and 5th Streets, in the heart of the Jewish neighborhood. My dad and his cousin Nate, Chaim's son, would tease the horse regularly, but only when it was tethered in the barn at the end of the day. The truth is, they were afraid of the old nag. When the horse finally died, Chaim could no longer work as a junkman.

Another neighbor, Mrs. Wolk, was in her nineties. She was no more than 4'8" tall, had sunken cheeks and no teeth. She too had a horse and wagon, and she would walk down the middle of the street, pulling her horse behind her, speaking Yiddish to it. A few days each week she would purchase fruit from a farmer, then walk down Penn Avenue with her horse and wagon, selling fruit to waiting families. There was no welfare back then, and Mrs. Wolk and her horse kept each other alive.

My aunt Rosie was one of her customers. Mrs. Wolk would stop at my aunt's house, water her horse, and get a cup of coffee and a piece of bread for herself. She and Aunt Rosie would speak Yiddish to each other while Mrs. Wolk dunked her bread into the coffee and gummed it down. No one

Ed Kreamer's college years.

Brother guided '35 DeSoto standing on running board

Article my dad wrote for the St. Louis Park Sun newspaper's Armistace Day paper November 1990—50 years later.

Armistice Day 1940 dawned dark and dreary with the temperature in the low 40s and raining with strong winds blowing.

My brother Jack and I drove to our college classes as usual. During the morning rumors began flying about a severe snow storm about to descend on us. Even from indoors we could hear the wind whistling and noted that the rain had turned to sleet and now to snow in extremely big and heavy flakes as the temperature began to drop very quickly.

Finally about 2 p.m. word came over the public address system that we were dismissed and to get home as soon as possible. A very severe snow storm was on the way. As my brother and I struggled to reach our car ('35 DeSoto) we knew that the announcement had been a gross understatement. The wind almost blew us away as we walked through ever bigger snow drifts.

We reached the car only to find the door lock frozen so we were unable to fit the key in. I walked to a nearby house and begged for an empty can, a candle and some matches. The

housewife demanded a quarter in payment, and my brother and I finally came up with 23 cents which she accepted. Back at the car, lighted candle (after many tries) shielded from the wind by the can, we got in and started "Old Faithful."

By this time everything was covered with so much snow and ice, it was almost impossible to know where the curb or the street actually was.

I had Jack stand up on the running board with his door open to direct me. In this manner, going about 5 to 10 miles per hour, we finally arrived at our back alley. My hope was to get it into the garage but as we plowed through the alley and aimed for the incline leading to our driveway, the car finally mired down and died in perhaps 18 inches to 2 feet of snow. My brother and I looked at each other, shrugged our shoulders and trudged our way into the house.

It was some 6 weeks later that we finally got the car towed out and sent to the repair shop.

E. Kreamer
St. Louis Park

Cars were caught in the snow storm in St. Louis Park on Excelsior Boulevard near Minikahda Golf Club (Minneapolis Tribune photo, reprinted with permission from the Minnesota Historical Society)

knew what the two woman talked about, but I think my aunt enjoyed her company.

My dad worked from the time he was 10 years old. His first job was delivering prescriptions for the pharmacist on the corner. His payment was one malted milk for every two deliveries.

My father also told me the story of the Armistice Day blizzard of 1941. No one had ever seen such a fast, furious snowfall. My dad was able to drive home from work in it, but all along the way he was stopping to help people out of snowbanks. He wound up getting stuck in the alley leading to his garage. It took days digging his car out of snow drifts to get his car to where it belonged.

My father graduated from North High School in 1930, 25 years before I did. When he celebrated his 50th class reunion, I was celebrating my 25th. Some of the same teachers were there for both of us.

After high school, my dad went to the University of Minnesota. He was the first in our family—including all his dozens of cousins from his seven aunts and two uncles—to attend college. He majored in German and was well on the way to becoming a German profes-

sor. Then World War II broke out. With Hitler as the leader in Germany, and what with the war and the rumors of what the Nazi's were doing to the Jews in Europe, my Dad felt that German was not what he should be studying. Why should he teach German, when the Germans hated him and others like him because of their Jewish identity? My father felt the only thing to do was quit college and go to business school.

Arnold Kreamer, Ed's brother during WWII

In just this way, many men of that time had their life goals totally rearranged by the overpowering, uncontrollable forces of World War II. (My father did, however, expect and insist that each of his three daughters get college educations—which we did, although I never finished. I, of course, expected and insisted that all my own children attend college and I hope you will do the same for yours.)

Both my father's younger brothers were drafted. During the war, my Uncle Jack was in the Navy, serving as a gunner aboard a ship in the Pacific. My Uncle Arnold served in the Army's ground forces as a paratrooper. My dad told me about the time Arnold was to be sent on a mission. He had no idea where he was going, but while he was standing in line to get into the transport plane, a man behind him saw some spots on his neck. The doctors checked it out and discovered he had developed measles. He was immediately quarantined. This saved him from taking part in the invasion of Okinawa-and may have saved his life.

Because of his birth defect, my father was not able to fight in the war or serve in the military. But he did what he could from home to help, both emotionally and financially, until his brothers returned. Everyone tightened their belts in the United States, and, fortunately, my uncles all came safely home after serving in the Pacific.

For the next few years after the war, my parents lived with my grandparents because, as Jews in the 1940s, they were not allowed to rent an apartment anywhere. But my dad worked hard at his job as an office manager for a very large wholesale carpet distributor. He dealt regularly with style and color, even though he was color blind all his life. (Color blindness is hereditary, and every first-born male in our family has this problem; women carry the gene, but do not have the condition.)

For not quite a year, my father and his brother Jack owned a delicatessen on Minneapolis' north side. Once, while slicing meat, my dad sliced part of his finger into the meat. But he just continued on with what he was doing as if nothing had happened, and no one was the wiser.

MINNEAPOLIS **JOURNAL**

MINNEAPOLIS, MINN, MOR... ...BE... 8, 1941

30 PAGES

Price 3 Cents

No.—No. 10

...S. DECLARES WAR ON JAPAN

3,000 Killed or Injured in Attack on Hawaii; 2 American Warships Sunk

Montana Woman Is Sole Dissenter; Senate Vote 82-0

Resolution Asked by President Roosevelt Speeded Through Congress in Strong Display of National Unity

WASHINGTON—Congress voted a formal declaration of war against Japan today after President Roosevelt requested immediate action as an answer to Japan's "unprovoked and dastardly attack" on Hawaii.

A united congress acted swiftly after the president had revealed American forces lost two warships and 1,000 dead and wounded in the surprise dawn attack yesterday.

Overwhelmingly and with the greatest unity shown in many a day on Capitol hill, the senate and house backed up President Roosevelt's request for a war declaration with unprecedented speed.

The senate vote to be recorded, was 82 to 0.
The house vote was 388 to 1.
The resolutions was before both houses within 15 minutes of the time Mr. Roosevelt ended his seven-minute, 500 ...

Japs Claim Huge Sea, Air Victory

American Warships Combing Pacific for Foe

MANILA—UP—Press dispatches ...

Britain De...
War on J...

Churchill Predicts and New Haven Dixon ...serts 'Hitler's Ma...

LONDON—UP—Britain ...
Japanese attack, declares ... ernment.

"It only remains ... cles to face their ... may give them."

At the same time ... free China.

BULLETINS

Axis, U. S. at War, Says Rome Radio

NEW YORK—UP—The Rome radio heard here, said ...

Vichy Reports Air-Sea Battle

NEW YORK—UP—The United Press listening post ...

Japanese Round Up British, Americans

TOKYO—UP—The Japanese ...

Belgians Recall Envoy in ...

Big Scale Naval Action Pushed in Reply to Tokyo

'Old Battleship' and Destroyer Lost, White House Reveals; Nippon Subs, Bombers Destroyed

WASHINGTON—(UP)—Casualties on the Hawaiian island of Oahu in Sunday's Japanese air attack will amount to about 3,000, including about 1,500 fatalities, the White House announced today.

The White House confirmed the loss in Pearl Harbor of "one old battleship" and a destroyer, which was blown up.

Several other American ships were damaged and a large number of army and navy airplanes on Hawaiian fields were put out of commission, the White House disclosed.

It reported that at the same time that AMERICAN OPERATIONS AGAINST JAPAN WERE BEING CARRIED OUT ON ¹ LARGE SCALE, ... DESTRUCTION ... NUMBER OF JAPANESE PLANES, AN...

Newspaper, December 8, 1941. Day after Hawaii was attacked; officially involving the U.S. into the theatre of war.

Monday, December 8, 1941

NEW YORK STOCKS

Noon Quotations

Neighborhood Theaters

EDINA — "THIS WOMAN IS MINE"

WESTGATE

BROADWAY — "DR. KILDARE'S WEDDING DAY"

PARK — "TEXAS"

HOLLYWOOD — Bud Abbott - Lou Costello — "HOLD THAT GHOST"

BRYNWOOD — ABBOTT & COSTELLO "HOLD THAT GHOST"

HOMEWOOD — "BARNACLE BILL"

EMPRESS — "SPOOKS RUN WILD"

ROXY — George Raft "MANPOWER"

AGATE — ABBOTT & COSTELLO "HOLD THAT GHOST"

ALHAMBRA

Primary

MAYOR
Two to be nominated
(205 Precincts out of 353)

T. A. Eide	19,971
Al. Hansen	5,801
Eugene R. (Jack) Kane	1,086
Marvin L. Kline	19,134
xGeorge E. Leach	15,196

THIRD WARD
(Complete)

xHenry H. Bank	4,156
Thomas E. Barbeau	218
Arthur B. Miller	371
Hy Ribnick	890
Otto H. Schuler	2,910

FOURTH WARD
(11 precincts out of 28)

xArthur B. Fruen	1,493
Arne Halonen	815
William E. (Bill) Honeycutt	780

APARTMENTS FOR RENT

FAIR OAKS

Better Values Than Ever!

Joslyn Realty — MA. 8133

APT. SEEKERS' GUIDE
L. L. HANSEN, INC.

WITH *Miracle*

Virginia Safford

STAGE WHISPERS: Carlton Miles, former Minneapolis dramatic critic, blew into town, then found he didn't have any work to do but look up some of his old friends. . After six years as advance man for "Tobacco Road," Carlton took over the same job this fall for Alfred Lunt and Lynn Fontanne. On arriving here he was informed they'd cancelled their local booking for "There Shall Be No Night" . . . The new Sigmund Romberg-Oscar Hammerstein operetta based on life in New Orleans in 1805, called "Sunny River," opened in New York last week with swell notices about our friend Bob Lawrence, who left the Curtis hotel to accept a singing role . . . Olsen and Johnson's "Sons O' Fun" also has hit Broadway . . . They'll probably stagger through another $5,000,000 success, ... them up.

It's a Fact
by HALSEY HALL

IT is a naturally assumed premise that we now shall all pull together to the common goal of victory and peace . . . It is a naturally assumed conclusion that everything is now "All-American," everyone is an All-American, everyone who does his or her bit to the fullest possible limit is eligible to the Most Valuable Player award . . . It also can be a naturally assumed fact

Charles Johnson's LOWDOWN ON SPORTS

IT WILL BE SOME TIME before anyone can say with any degree of accuracy what effect the war with Japan will have on sports generally from a competitive as well as an attendance standpoint.

Naturally, it will make heavy inroads here and there, but it isn't likely that sport programs will be cancelled although a curtailment is likely all the way down the line.

IN THIS CORNER
with Cedric Adams

NATIONAL EFFICIENCY in a national crisis such as yesterday is indicated by the fact that exactly four hours after the Pacific doings had popped, the FBI had instructed every aviation unit in Minneapolis that has private planes for rent, hire or sale that no Japanese could become a customer from then on. It's rather gratifying to Mr. and Mrs. Joe Citizen to see just a single little detail like that carried out with such startling dispatch . . . Flying and Popular Aviation magazine hit the bull's-eye with a nifty piece of timing—its entire January issue is given over to naval aviation, exactly the kind of warfare that probably will draw the emphasis in the Pacific . . . Local Angle: First radio

My parents met in North Minneapolis through one of my dad's cousins, Dorothy Lehrman. They were married December 13, 1941, after a two-year courtship. When they married, Dad was 24 and Mom was 21.

Every day throughout their entire first year of marriage, my dad brought home a single red rose for Mom. The following year, he brought her a slice of pie each day from the Normandy Hotel restaurant. (He would check with the restaurant to find out when the pies would come out of the oven, so that his Rosie would have a nice, fresh piece. My dad worked in St. Paul then, and he would drive home through downtown Minneapolis every day for that special piece of pie for his special lady. Her favorite, Boston Creme, remained her favorite until the day she died.)

My dad was raised in an era of male dominance: women stayed at home, men made a living. He was the pampered first child who was taken care of all his young life; after he met my mother, she took care of him in the same fashion.

My dad was not a very demonstrative man. Yet my memory serves me well, and I remember that he was caring in a number of ways. He read poetry to me at night before I went to bed. He

My dad Ed Kreamer holding Sandy in 1943

would take me and my younger sister Bitsy on long summer hikes through the Eloise Butler Preserve, not far from our house. He would use a walking stick, and it made us feel as though we had walked miles when we were done. We would stop for a drink from the natural spring that ran through the preserve, and we had to pump at the water by hand, making us feel like pioneers.

Dad also taught me to fish. I was the only girl in the neighborhood who would bait my own hook, take the fish off the hook, and then clean and scale it. Poking at their eyes-so round and smooth-fascinated me, although I could never get them out of their heads.

My father was very bright, and he loved reading, good conversation, and great debates. Nevertheless, he was a soft-spoken man who chose his words carefully and was very dedicated to his family. (Yet I always feared his temper, which would flare whenever he was frustrated by my behavior.)

He always hoped to have a son, and with each of my mother's pregnancies he would call upon Rabbi Shepsul, the moyel, telling him the expected date of the birth and the planned date for the bris. But the time for a bris never came for him: he had three daughters.

This story has a happy ending, however. With the birth of my son Stephen in January of 1965, I proudly gave my father the pleasure of making that call to the moyel and setting the date for his grandson's bris.

When I was in the hospital after Stephen's birth, my dad came to visit me every day. One day he saw that I was feeling a little blue, so he immediately went home and came back with an assortment of 1940s hats he still owned. He walked in wearing one, talked with me for a bit, then left and came back in with a different one on. He kept doing this, over and over, each time with another old hat, worn in a different way or at a different angle, until I started laughing so much that I cried.

Not that my dad didn't appreciate his granddaughters. He loved all his grandchildren. When Tara was a baby, each morning my dad would drive to my house. I would run around the lakes with my friends early in the morning, and Dad would wait for Tara to get up from her night's sleep. He would change her diaper and make hot cocoa for her, which she always looked forward to. When I returned after an hour and a half, both of them would be watching for me to come home, Tara in one large chair and her Papa in another. I can still hear her laughter coming through the huge picture window. Dad retired the year Tara arrived; he told his fellow employees he was retiring to take care of his newest grandchild.

He had a wonderful, dry sense of humor. He would make up clever sayings, and I never knew what he would come up with next. (Once, as he was explaining something to me, he said, "On the other hand, there are five fingers.")

One of the saddest moments of my life came one Passover, but it is tinged with humor because of my dad. It was April of 1997, and our family knew Mom, who was ill with Alzheimer's, would probably not see another Pesach. I held a large seder at my house for the whole family, and my dad came equipped with many different colored

yarmulkes (skullcaps) to wear at the table while conducting services. Every time one of us would look up at him, he would have quickly changed caps without anyone noticing, and he would act as if nothing had changed. He wanted us to have some happy memories of this Passover as well as sad ones.

Throughout his life, Dad carried himself with much pride and dignity. He was always an honest, very hard-working man. When my mother was diagnosed with Alzheimer's Disease in

From left to right, three brothers, Arnold, Ed and Jack in 1991

1988, he became her caregiver, and he did a far better job than anyone else I could ever imagine. He cared for her lovingly for eight years before her death in 1998.

For nearly all of his adult life, Rose had taken care of him. Now the roles became reversed. My dad became the sole cook and bottle washer. He made great salads, good hamburgers, and some of the best chicken soup I have ever tasted; quite a feat for someone who had had his dinner cooked for him for the past 50 years.

My father's caring and compassion also gave me and my sisters a sense of security. Even though we helped as much as we could, we always knew that our dad was with Mom, caring for her and loving her with unconditional patience. He took her to her favorite places—the ones she loved and was familiar with. At least once a week they would go to the art museum, to have lunch and explore. Every day they would go antiquing, shopping, or at least out for lunch.

I don't mean that he never got frustrated with her—in fact, sometimes the two would get into arguments. But I would be the luckiest woman in the world if I were to find someone to share the last quarter of my life with who is as caring and loving as my dad.

Rose Kreamer - My Mother

My mother and her one sister were born at home above the creamery. Rose came into this world on July 13, 1920. As the youngest, "baby" became the nickname used by family and friends.

Rose had a wonderful, innocent childhood, which included a lot of friends. She was a total free spirit, not at all shy. She loved sitting on the steps of the general store and listening to the opera on the radio on Saturday afternoons. In high school she was very popular and was a cheerleader for the school's great football team.

Mom told me all about my grandmother's good cooking. Everything was made from scratch, including the bread she'd bake for Friday night meals. The family always ate their main meal at lunch,

Rose Kreamer

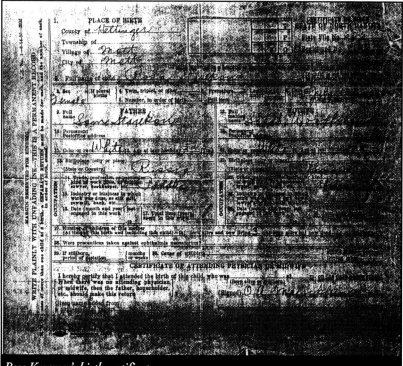

Rose Kreamer's birth certificate

Rose Kreamer

which Grandpa Sam would come home for. Their evening meal was a light one.

There was never any talk of not having enough of anything. The Great Depression of the 1930s never touched her family. There was always food on the table and newly handmade clothes when needed. But Rose didn't like it that her mother made all her clothes. She wanted to buy her clothes at the store like her girlfriends.

In my mother's later years, she told me that her family had been harassed by the Ku Klux Klan, and that KKK members had physically hurt her dad. She never told us the whole story, though. It must have required a lot to be able to detach from the pain, fear, and helplessness of that terrible experience.

The tragedy of my grandfather's sudden drowning was also understandably traumatic for her. In fact, the shock caused her to stop menstruating, and at age sixteen she was told she would never have children.

When my mother was seventeen and a senior in high school, her family moved to Minneapolis. The move was very difficult for her, and in some ways she never got over it. For her it was a nightmare: moving to a large city, going to a large city school, not knowing anyone, and, worst of all, no one knowing her. She had gone all through school with the same friends for eleven years. She had to lose her small town innocence, with no guidance. My mother's older siblings had grown up and moved on in their lives. It was just my mom and her mother living together. Imagine a woman who spoke very little English, and a teenage girl who knew no one in the strange big city she suddenly found herself thrust into. This was a very frightening time for Rose...until she met my father.

She was introduced to Ed Kreamer through a friend she met at school, Dorothy Lehrman. Dorothy was my dad's cousin and Rose Meltzer's daughter. (Rose M. was one of my grandmother's sisters-my great aunt. Rose M. was also Grandma Tina's oldest sister.)

My parents met when my mother Rose was eighteen and Ed was 21. It was quite a memorable day, not only for Rose and Ed, but for the people who introduced them. My dad had just gotten home from having his tonsils removed. He loved all the attention and sympathy he was getting, so he did his best to show everyone the great pain he was enduring. His cousin Dorothy, one of the first friends my mother made after moving to Minneapolis, happened to be with Rose that day, and they decided to visit Ed. When they arrived, Dorothy introduced Rose and Ed to each other. Ed put a special look of pain on his face and let out a moan.

Then, a moment later, while looking at Ed, Dorothy felt something sliding down her back. It was Rose, who had fainted: she thought Ed was dying. My father later said that as soon as he took his first look at Rose, he knew that she was the woman he was going to marry. And my mother told me that before she dropped to the ground, she too knew that Ed was the man for her.

They courted for about a year before Ed asked Rose to marry him, and they tied the knot in Minneapolis on December 13, 1941. Their modest honeymoon was spent in St. Paul.

Marriage certificate of Ed and Rose Kreamer

It was a true love match, but a turbulent filled marriage none-the-less. To everyone's surprise, Rose became pregnant with me during the first year of their marriage. I was considered a gift, but I was also a symbol. My dad's brothers were in the Pacific fighting in the war. I, the first grandchild and the first niece, would become the symbol in our family of what they were fighting for: the peace and safety of future generations.

Peace was a major concern of my mother's for much of her life. During the Vietnam War she was a committed peacenik, marching and demonstrating in Minneapolis to get our boys out of Vietnam. In 1971, she and her dear friend Ruth Balto decided that they would have more of an impact if they went to Washington, DC, and joined with other marchers from all over the United States. So on April 15, 1971, these two little Jewish ladies from north Minneapolis found themselves outside the White House, yelling and chanting anti-war slogans. I have never been as proud of my mom as I was during that time.

My mother was always very liberal, and she believed in honesty and love between people. She could never understand inequality and was pained by all the unfairness, poverty, and despair in this world. She would stop to give money to homeless people and street musicians, and she would stop to talk to any baby she saw on the street. I was often afraid that some fearful parent would think my mom was a little loony and call the police, but this never happened-for which I am thankful.

Rose taught her daughters honesty, love, and the meaning of "There but for the grace of God go I." For many years she had a number of children around the world whom she gave money to every month. (She had a drawer full of pictures of the kids she was helping.) I wish the world was as sensitive as she was to others' pain.

In 1985, for my mother's 65th birthday, I took her for a weekend in Manhattan. We went to see *Madame Butterfly* at the Metropolitan Opera, to fulfill a dream she had always had from the time she would listen to the opera over the radio as a child. We shared the excitement of Manhattan—catching cabs, having high tea at the Ritz, and seeing a great play, *I'm Not Rappaport*. We talked and laughed and walked the streets of New York together.

One of the last wonderful moments she shared with us was Stephen's wedding on June 8, 1997, when she was almost 77. (She would not be diagnosed with lung cancer for three more months.) At the end of the ceremony, as the bride and groom walked back up the aisle, she jumped up and kissed them both with tears in her eyes. Afterward, she danced the night away.

Rose Kreamer's death was one of the most spiritual times I have ever shared with others. The beauty in which she passed away, surrounded by her family and friends, is a tribute to her and to how she wanted to share all she had with those she loved.

She lay in bed, slowly dying for five days, while each of us said goodbye. The hospice nurses kept her aware but in no pain by feeding her morphine whenever she got a little agitated.

We soothed her, kissed her, and hugged her day and night. We would not let her die alone, and she knew we were always there. It was much like experiencing a birth.

She held onto her good humor to the end. When my sister Bitsy leaned over Mom's bed and told her that she would take care of Dad, Mom replied in a low, weak voice, "Lucky you." When the nurses turned her from one side to another, she whispered, "Make up your mind."

My son Stephen and his wife Julie flew into Minneapolis to be near her at the end. When Stephen first walked into her bedroom and said, "Grandma, it's me, Stephen," she raised her arm to hug him and said, "My darling." Then she pointed downstairs to her basement, reminding him to take the boxes he had stored there years earlier. She had nagged him for years to remove them, and even as her life neared its end she hadn't forgotten.

My youngest daughter, Tara, was remarkable. She stayed home from school all five days to sit with her "little Grammy." Shortly before Rose became unresponsive, Tara and her friends brought her flowers and a declaration of their love in a beautiful note. Tara also gave me a sealed letter to put in my mother's coffin, and made me promise that I would never read it.

After Rose had lapsed into a coma, Tara and her friends simply sat there with her, holding her. I asked them what they were doing, and they answered, "We're just sitting and chillin' out with Gram." She knew that hearing is the last of the senses to go, and I knew they wanted her to hear that they were there.

My mom was the most beautiful and giving soul that God placed on this Earth. She loved all people and all things. She felt each of her grandchildren was a special gift to her, and she loved each one for who they were. At her funeral, the rabbi spoke of her love of animals, which was so great that she would house stray cats in her garage, and make my dad buy straw in the winter to help them stay warm.

Two weeks before she died, she sat at my kitchen table with my dad and me, having a cup of tea. I had just finished polishing my nails bright red, and I polished hers the same color so we would be twins. I made sure to do a great job, because I knew how proud my mother was, how nice she wanted to look, and how she never lost her dignity, no matter what happened.

She died with the same polish on. She will wear one of the last things I did for her into eternity, forever in peace.

Rose has left me a wonderful legacy, and I hope someday to have a few grandchildren of my own to pass on the wonderful stories of my mom, my children's Grandma Rose.

Northeast Chapel 378-1331

Kreamer

Rose and Ed Kreamer last Hanukah (before she died Jan 9, 1998), December 28, 1997 at Lisa's house.

Rose, age 77, of St. Louis Park, died January 9 after a courageous battle with lung cancer. Born July 13, 1920 in Mott, N.D. Preceded in death by parents, Sam & Sarah Starekow; brother, Milton; & sister, Hattie Marofsky. Survived by husband, Edward; daughters, Sandy, Bitsy, Rachel; grandchildren, Stephen & Julie Winer, Lisa & Brett Scholder, Tara Lynn Winer; many nieces and nephews; 2 brothers-in-law and their families; and many wonderful and caring friends and relatives; and loving puppy, Tippy III. A special thanks to all the wonderful HealthSpan Hospice care givers who made the process a beautiful and easier one. Funeral Services SUNDAY, 12 Noon, Hodroff & Sons Funeral Chapel, 126 East Franklin Ave. In lieu of flowers memorials preferred to the Mpls Institute of Art or the donor's favorite charity. SHIVA 2561 Oregon Ave. S.

Two

Sandy Kreamer-
Growing up
on Minneapolis'
North Side

In the year I was born, 1943, America was at war in Europe. Hitler was in power, exterminating Jews in the European countries he controlled. Meanwhile, anti-Semitism was running rampant here in the United States as well. In 1943 in Minneapolis, Jews were fighting their own local war against anti-Semitism.

Jews from all parts of the world had immigrated to Minnesota and settled in the north side of the city. This grouping together for safety and security was part of the shtetl mentality. Most of the German Jews had immigrated to the United States during the end of the 19th century. The Russian Jews came later, after 1910. Most of the Jewish families living on the north side were from Russia or Poland, while the Jewish families from Germany and Austria settled mostly in south Minneapolis. (There was prejudice among both groups. The German Jews thought of the Russians as "the other Jews," and that's how I thought of them.)

Our family is descended from the hard-working second wave of Jewish immigrants. These were generally tailors and shopkeepers rather than scholars, though they were equally bright. They did not have the advantages of extensive schooling, however.

On March 7, 1943, I came screaming into the world at Maternity Hospital, not far from where most of Minneapolis' Jewish community lived. At the time, Maternity was one of only two hospitals in the Twin Cities

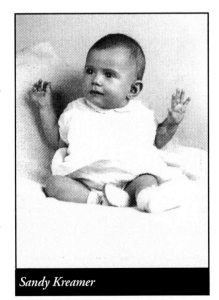

Sandy Kreamer

where Jewish patients were admitted or Jewish doctors were allowed to practice medicine. (The Jewish community dealt with this problem about a decade later, by building a Jewish hospital, called Mt. Sinai, with money raised from local Jewish families.)

That March brought horrid weather, and I was born in the middle of a raging snowstorm which closed many roads. The only way my dad could come see his newborn daughter was to walk three or four miles each way through a blinding snowstorm and freezing temperatures. But he did it.

When my parents took me home from the hospital, it was to my grandmother Tina's house. My parents were living there because they couldn't find rental housing for us. Since Minneapolis was such a hotbed of anti-Semitism, almost no one would rent to Jews.

Finally, when I was six months old, my parents were able to rent an apartment off Highway 55 (Olson Memorial Drive), in the community simply called the Projects. These were apartment buildings filled with newly married, and not so well-to-do young couples; basically Jews and blacks. It was Minneapolis' version of a ghetto. This was right after the end of World War II, and many people in the Projects were new families headed by servicemen who had just come home. I have many happy memories of my early years there.

In the Projects, my parents met many of their life-long friends, including Ann and Taffy Dachis, and Doris Goldberg and her husband Frank. These people all felt like one giant family to me.

My most vivid memory during my early years in the Projects is when my mother, as she sent me out to play with my friends, gave me this stern warning: "Sandy, never call a black person a nigger." Of course, I wanted to see what lesson there was to learn from this. The first thing I did when I saw a black child outdoors was call him a nigger. To this day I can remember him chasing me all the way home. I was frightened for my life and felt very lucky that I made it home alive. I never told my parents what happened, and I never used that word again.

Sandy Kreamer with her parents in front of the projects in 1945

In the mornings I went to a neighborhood nursery school in the Phyllis Wheatley House. The school, Harriet Tubman Nursery School, was named after a black woman who had helped many slaves escape to the North during the middle of the 19th century. In the afternoons after school, I played with neighborhood friends.

What I remember most from my early years was summer. On summer nights, we would sit on the stoops of our houses and listen to the electric buzz of the cicadas and the hubbub of other insects. Men would be on their after-dinner walks, speaking different European dialects of Yiddish. After the dinner dishes were done, women would start to straggle slowly out from their houses "to catch a breeze" and visit with neighbors. (There was no air conditioning for us back then.) The evening would end with us being called in to our baths and bedtimes. Life was simple and sweet.

I remember trying to sleep at night with my head resting on the window ledge, hoping to feel a cool breeze. Outside, I would hear Dad watering the lawn by hand with a hose and kids playing baseball or hide and seek in the dark. I would try to feel some wind while listening to the cicadas and crickets talking. Nights seemed endless during some of those unbearable July and August heat waves.

Eventually, though, September would arrive. There would be a chill in the air, and everyone would rake up all their leaves, put them in big barrels in their yards, and burn them. For me, one sure sign that Fall had come was that sharp smell of burning leaves.

This was a very secure, safe time for us all. No one had to lock their doors, and we slept with the windows wide open. We had the freedom to play in the streets day or night. On any one block in north Minneapolis there were people we knew or were related to. Family was always around us, and all of us shared our trials and tribulations. Some adult always knew what I was up to, which definitely made it hard to get into trouble—but I always managed to, anyway.

When I was three I developed pneumonia. One lung would not clear, and I was taken to the hospital. The oral medication they gave me didn't work, and I became so sick I nearly died. I wound up staying there for three months. For one of those months I was quarantined, unable to see my parents. They were only able to look at me through the window of my hospital room.

Specialists came from all over the city to examine me. They did not think I would live, but wanted to remove the infected lung. Fortunately, my pediatrician refused to allow them to.

Finally they decided to try something new. Every other day I would be delivered to the operating room to have my lungs drained with needles, and inject penicillin directly into them. I still remember being alone, afraid, and near death, looking into the nurses' faces as they wheeled me down to surgery.

After a few weeks of the injections, I finally began to rally. My fever subsided, and my parents became hopeful that I would live. Fortunately, I did not have my lung removed.

My fourth birthday was spent with the nurses and doctors, and I was told that I was the longest-staying patient the hospital had.

While I was in the hospital my mother gave birth (in another hospital) to my sister Bitsy. It was a very difficult time for my parents, who had to bring a new daughter into the world while another lay in a hospital bed, on the verge of death.

Most of my memories of the time are happy ones, however. For instance, each summer a man would come to our neighborhoods with a few Shetland ponies for us to ride. They would be tethered to a pole in the center of a circle, and for a few cents I would ride in circles on top of these seemingly giant beasts, my feet in stirrups and a cowboy hat on my head. I thought it was great.

Back then, north Minneapolis was largely a community of Jewish cooks. Every household had one. The foods and meals were basically the same, but each household prepared them a little differently, depending upon which part of the old world their grandparents or parents immigrated from. Every home had a different smell, but it was still the smell of borscht, kugel, and flanken. I remember walking by people's open windows during warm weather and smelling all their cooking. In winter, when the windows were closed, they were covered with steam from the cooking.

We were kept warm by chicken soup on Fridays and barley soup during the rest of the week. We had stews cooked with fresh potatoes, delicious kosher meat, and tons of carrots, celery, and onions. It would all cook slowly, and the wonderful, mouth-watering smell of natural juices would fill our kitchen and waft into our bedrooms while we were doing our homework. Our kitchen always felt warm, even though our bedrooms were freezing. (In those days it was thought to be healthier if you slept in the cold.)

One memory I'll never forget is breakfast on winter mornings. My mom would cook hot cereal, usually Cream of Wheat or Malt-O-Meal, and toast to fill our stomachs and warm us up before school. I would love the smell of the cereal cooking on the stove—a warm, smooth, soft smell that invited us into the kitchen. I almost didn't mind waking on cold mornings, because I'd be welcomed by the smell. It would be pitch black outside, but then I'd go into the kitchen with all the lights on and all the breakfast smells, and my dad would be sitting at the table listening to the news on WCCO,

"The Good Neighbor to the North," and eating. (Growing up, I almost never saw my parents go to sleep or wake up. I only saw them in other rooms in our home, always awake and always fully dressed.)

❦

Although almost all my memories involving food are pleasant, my very first food-related memory is of vomiting up cauliflower. I was forced to eat it because it was good for me, and I was not permitted to leave the table until I finished it. I hated it though, and my parents were surprised when I gave it back to them in a very different form.

Then there was the time I got into poison rhubarb. Long ribbons of rhubarb lined the alleyways behind the houses in north Minneapolis. They grew wild and free, and since no one took notice or care of them, I figured no one owned them and they were mine to eat. So I ate myself full, and then barfed it all back out.

I was always going into neighbors' yards for rhubarb, apples, plums—anything edible—and eating my fill. To my parents, though, this was stealing so when they found me vomiting over and over, I was too afraid to tell them why.

I had one other traumatic moment during my earliest years: when I was in nursery school I got hit by a school bus. The school bus driver let me off in front of my building and told me to walk around the front of the bus. He thought I had already made it to the curb, and he started on his way again but I was so small that he couldn't see me. The bus hit me, and I can still vividly remember the shock and pain. I tried crawling out from under the bus, but couldn't make it to the curb. The bus driver felt me under his wheels and stopped immediately, which probably saved my life. My mother heard the noise, looked out her window, and saw a stranger lifting me from the ground and carrying me into the building.

Doctors made house calls back then. When the doctor arrived, he gave me a thorough exam, washed me off, and told my mom that I had no broken bones and would be okay. But I still carry faint scars above my right eye, from where the wheels of the bus hit my head, reminding me of the scars my grandfather Isadore had.

***

We lived in the Projects until the summer before I entered kindergarten. At that time my parents bought a duplex at 1315 Queen Avenue North with my Uncle Jack and Aunt Reva. Each family paid, approximately, $1,000. That's right-the total purchase price for the whole building was $2,000. We lived downstairs and Reva and Jack lived upstairs.

Our two families were very close. In the summer, Uncle Jack and I would sit on the back stairs and eat watermelon, seeing how far we could spit the seeds. On most Sundays, all of us would have a light dinner at our house: eggs, cottage cheese, tomatoes, bagels, and smoked fish.

Big, old oak and maple trees lined the streets and sidewalks of our neighborhood. Their huge roots cracked and pushed up the sidewalks around their bases. This made the sidewalk almost hilly, and fun to bike or roller skate over. We used the sidewalks for hop-scotch, and the trees became bases in our neighborhood baseball games. They were also great for hiding in during moonlit games of hide and seek on warm summer evenings.

In the early morning hours when I would rise, I'd hear the low, almost trance-like cooing of pigeons. Their sound was very comforting, and they told us the day had begun. Nowadays you don't hear them much.

Before my first school year began, my dad would walk me to the school several times, and we'd look into the windows of the classrooms. He was trying to familiarize me with my first big leap out into this big world. He had gone to the same school as a child and wanted me to see that it wasn't as frightening as I imagined it would be. As a result, my school felt as safe as my home to me even before I started in September.

Projects where I lived as they look today in 1997 before they were to be torn down

Summer library on highway 55 and Emerson Ave. North, my dad always took me.

Hospital I took my first breath in—3/7/43—on corner of Glenwood Avenue and Penn Avenue North, Minneapolis, Minnesota

Willard Elementary School on Queen Avenue North where my elementary school years were spent.

Todmud Tarah Hebrew school I graduated from—directly across from Willard school

I spent 7-9th grades at Lincoln Jr. High—on Penn Avenue North in Minneapolis.

I attended Willard School, the nearby public elementary school. (It's still up and running, carrying the same name.) We would walk home for lunch every day, where my mother would have a hot lunch waiting for us. (There was no hot lunch program in school.) An hour later, we were back in school. If the weather was so bad that it was hard to get home for lunch, we would be allowed to bring our lunches and eat in our classrooms. But our duplex was only four blocks from school, making it easy for me to make it no matter what the weather was like.

At that time we had six synagogues on the north side, all within walking distance of our home. You could feel the religious atmosphere in the streets and playgrounds, in the shops and schools. There were so many Jewish kids in my school that on Jewish holidays the teachers couldn't teach because each class would have only three or four kids attending. The rest of us were in synagogue.

Across the street from Willard was the Hebrew school which I attended. My classmates and I would run across the street after school, have milk and chocolate chip cookies (which the Hebrew school sold), study Hebrew for two hours, and then walk home.

I remember being afraid of dogs while walking to school and back. My Grandma Tina worried about dogs, too. I remember that she would watch me walking to school to protect me from any dogs that might bother me. But she would hide behind a tree so my mother wouldn't see her watching for me. She didn't do this every day, but it made me feel very safe and protected.

Grandma Tina hid because my mother didn't want her watching out for me in that way. She was determined to raise independent girls. When she discovered what Tina was doing, she was furious. (She did help us all learn to be independent, though. It took me over forty years to understand what she was trying to do for me and my sisters.)

All the neighbors my mother had as friends became my aunts, and I called them all "Aunty" before their names. Their husbands were never my uncles, though, because they were almost never around, like most men then. Very hard work and long hours kept just about all our fathers away from home, and when they would be home, they were unapproachable. Most fathers were kept well protected by their wives back then. That was the housewives' job: to make the home nice and to keep it peaceful for their husbands, who worked all day to support their families.

As kids, we had to show absolute respect for our fathers, a respect that bordered on fear. Our fathers were kept distant from us, and we never got to know who our fathers were, what they thought, or what they felt. They were not to be questioned. At dinner every night, we could not speak until we were spoken to first. As a result, my sisters and I would always get into trouble at the table for attention.

My parents were not poor. We always had whatever we needed, and our home was furnished like all my friends' houses—brown in color and very practical, without much imagination. Of course, no computers, typewriters, or fax machines graced our home; at that time, computers were first being experimented with, and each one was so large it filled an entire room.

My parents—Bitsy sitting with dad; Sandy on right, mom on left

Mom and dad, Bitsy and me on a family vacation in front of our cabin

Friends in the park l. to r. back: Sandy, Linda Israel, front: Fern Yellen, Bitsy Kreamer, Gail Israel

In front of our duplex l. to r. Bitsy, Sandy, cousin Joel on lap and cousin Sherie

My sister Bitsy age 4; I was 8 years old.

Sister Bitsy's birthday in our home standing in back l. to r. Gail Israel and Fern Yellen; seated: Bitsy and Sheri Kreamer, Sandy Kreamer and Linda Israel sitting together.

Sandy in center, cousin Sheri Kreamer left, Bitsy, my sister, in 1954

Family picnic, realtives around picnic table, sandy and cousins in forefront

On a picnic with cousin Robin Meltzer at Minnehaha Falls Park

Pearl Tina Isadore Gertie

Bitsy, Cheri, Joel

Picnic Birthday party for Sheri Kreamer, May 1958

Spry

Family picnic, Sandy, Bitsy, family friend Hedy Levy, and dad, Ed behind the thermos

Picnic at Lake Harriet— Papa in forefront, Tina to his left, I'm in front of my dad and Bitsy's in front of grandma Tina, Tina's sisters and husbands against the tree, Aunt Jessie and husband in front of them, Aunt Lily, her husband and Aunt Pearl on the end

Each home I lived in when I was growing up had only one bathroom. Yet there was never an argument over it, because everyone growing up in that time period was taught to share.

❦

My sister Elizabeth Ann, always called Bitsy, was born four years after I was, on January 23, 1947. Bitsy and I were always very close, and I could do almost anything with her or to her. I would pound on her when I got angry, but also played Indians with her. We would crawl into the same bed together, hold a blanket high over our heads, and speak like the Indians did on the TV shows. We also comforted each other when we would hear our parents arguing.

I remember Bitsy being sent from the dinner table because we couldn't stop giggling. I felt terrible and started worrying about her.

Bitsy Kreamer, 7 months old 1947

I put mashed potatoes in my pocket, claimed I had to go the bathroom, and brought the potatoes to her so she wouldn't starve. (On other evenings, I'd throw food across the table at her.)

For a while Bitsy and I had bunk beds. My parents bought them to save space, but all it got us were a couple of good knocks on our heads when we would fall from the top bunk. Finally they decided our brains were more important than sleeping space, and they turned them into two free-standing twin beds for us.

Sometimes our parents would leave the two of us alone, with me in charge. Then we would always cook. We made fudge that never hardened, hard-boiled eggs for sandwiches, and chocolate pudding. We thought we were great chefs, until Mom would come back and re-cook our fudge or re-boil our eggs. We also made a lot of mashed potatoes, which I loved. In fact, I still love all these foods, and to this day I make them as comfort foods.

After World War II, everyone was starting families, and I think some of them forgot to stop. There were dozens and dozens of kids to play with. We didn't worry about the ages of our playmates. It was just a question of what you wanted to do and finding some who would do it with you. We'd bike, roller skate, shoot marbles, or play hospital. Bitsy and I were always running around the neighborhood, playing and eating at everyone else's house—sometimes having another meal after our own.

Rachel Maxine, my baby sister, was born seven years after Bitsy, on January 21, 1954. She was a very cute and cuddly baby, with beautiful reddish golden curls. I was almost twelve years old when she was born, and in my mind she became my baby. I loved her as if she was my own child, and I was always taking her with me and my friends. I baby-sat her regularly, and cared for her with the best of my young abilities. I would take her out for ice cream, and when I had my first job, the first present I bought with my earnings was a beautiful imported doll for Rachel. I would also bring her books and other gifts, hoping she would save them and remember me. That eleven year difference felt like an eternity.

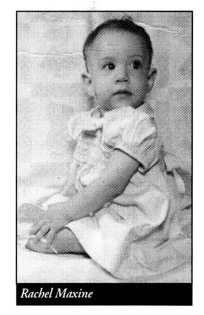

Rachel Maxine

To most of the world, including my parents and grandparents, I was Sandy, but Bitsy and Rachel called me Sam.

During these years I felt very secure, very safe. Our home was not expensively furnished, but it was filled with memorable pieces of furniture.

The old family kitchen table we had back then is now back in style. It was the plastic-topped, chromed-legged kind with matching plastic seat covers on the chairs. If only we had saved it! We ate off Fiestaware—the same stuff that is now selling again in department stores as something cool and modern.

The living room was the warmest, most comforting room in our house, and in it was a special piece of furniture: the big, soft, wonderful sofa. I would get the honor of lying on it, all wrapped in blankets, when I stayed home sick from school. I remember it being very large—almost the size of my twin bed—and feeling comforted, as if I were being cradled in a pair of loving arms. Our only TV was in the living room, and it was my entertainment while getting well. That small back and white Motorola gave me a little window into the world. Sometimes I'd get up early, blurry-eyed, turn on the TV, and watch test patterns, waiting for the television day to begin. News would come on at seven, then the farm news, then my beloved cartoon characters: Casper the Friendly Ghost, Rocky and Bullwinkle, and a host of others. Casey Jones came into the living room in his train at lunch time to share a sandwich with us, all the while telling us jokes that kids sent to him. Then he'd show us more cartoons. (After Casey, it was my mother's turn for the TV and her soap operas.)

The big easy chair next to the sofa in the living room was for my dad. But for most of the evening his favorite place was at the kitchen table, where he would read the newspaper until the ten o'clock news. Then he would join my mother in front of the TV.

When Dad wasn't in the big chair, Bitsy and I would sometimes fight over it. Cartoons were always best when you watched them in the big chair. If one of us was using it and had to leave for a minute, she would always make sure the others knew she was coming back and that it was still hers.

Our most important item of furniture, though, was the dining room table. Our whole family gathered around it every Friday night for the best meal of the week. That meal was always prepared from scratch. Nothing was pre-cooked, and we never ate TV dinners. Even cake mixes were unheard of in our house.

Our family life in the late 40s and 50s revolved around meals. They were always eaten only at the dining room or kitchen table, with the whole family in attendance. We would always wait for Dad to come home from the office, or from synagogue, no matter what the time or how much our stomachs complained.

In my mother's home, food and its preparation were as simple as the times. Dinner was always a full four-course meal, with salad, meat (often meatloaf), potatoes (usually mashed), and a vegetable. Although my mother made almost everything from scratch, the vegetables were often from cans. If we ate all that was served to us, dessert was our prize. It was almost always homemade cake, pie, or cookies.

I loved watching my mother make her mashed potatoes. She'd put the boiled potatoes through a colander-like kitchen utensil called a ricer. To make sure there were no lumps in her potatoes, she'd squash them through, and they would come out the bottom, wiggling like worms.

Our Friday nights meals were usually eaten in our dining room. Challah was the focus of our attention, and dipping it in the chicken soup and sucking the soup from the bread was a deeply sensual experience for me. I couldn't tell you which tasted better, the soup or the bread. Both were freshly made that same day. Everything was placed on my mother's best tablecloth, and God forbid we should spill a drop. On Friday evenings my sisters and I knew to behave, and we used our best manners.

When my mother started having Passover in her not-too-large home, we would set the table for 25 people. The table only seated twelve, but it was always dragged out into the living room, and a smaller table was added on at the end. When everyone arrived, we had nowhere to stand, so we would immediately sit down at the table to wait until the last guest arrived. The door was always open, not only to let Elijah in, but because of the heat in the house from all the bodies and all the cooking.

On Saturday afternoons, the most reliable and popular babysitter for all the children in north Minneapolis was the Homewood Theater. It provided respite for our parents and lots of fun for us. For the sum of 25 cents we would spend all afternoon in the movie house, which would be filled with all our friends. For our quarters we would get ten cartoons, five continuing serials, and then a full-length movie (Tarzan was my all-time favorite). On top of all this, a man would walk on stage and call out numbers. If one of the numbers matched the one on your ticket stub, you would win a whole bag of groceries.

I have often wondered what my parents did while we were at the Homewood. Now that I have raised children of my own, I understand how precious those child-free Saturday afternoons must have been for them.

When I was eight, my mother took me to my first evening movie. It was Calamity Jane-a musical with Doris Day, in color. The theater looked no different that night, but I felt proud when I looked around and realized that I was the only child in the audience. I felt very grown up, and at that moment I knew I had arrived. Staying up past my normal bedtime was the high point of my evening.

I remember shopping in small grocery stores with my mother. There were no chain stores. Sometimes she would call her favorite store in the neighborhood to place her order, and they would deliver the food that same day. We got most of our groceries from the Knox Grocery Store on Knox and Plymouth Avenues.

There were little corner grocery stores every few blocks down the avenue where we lived. They were good places for buying candy, gum, and packages of trading cards. These were like baseball cards, except that in those days there were all kinds of different subjects. I collected cards of cats, dogs, flowers, and horses.

When we wanted ice cream, we always went down to the drugstore on the corner, Desnick's Drugs. We would get wonderful ice cream cones for a nickel. Malts and huge sundaes were twenty-five cents. Turtle sundaes were my favorite, with loads of hot fudge on three scoops of ice cream. It was all topped off with nuts, whipped cream, and that perfect bright red cherry with the long stem.

At Desnick's our family got prescriptions, ice cream, cigarettes, cigars, and candy bars. My friends and I loved hanging out on the corner in front of Desnick's after school and on summer nights. When my sister Bitsy was old enough, she got her first job at Desnick's.

The delicatessens in my neighborhood were plentiful. At Plitman's Del, the closest deli to my house, my favorite meal was their kosher hot dog in a bun with plenty of mustard, and baked beans on the side. (Try the recipe for baked beans on forthcoming pages. They're delicious, though they don't have exactly the same flavor of Plitman's. I asked the people at Plitman's for their recipe, but they would never divulge their secret.) Sadly, all the north side delis have been gone for many years now.

Our meat was always kosher, purchased from one of the many kosher butcher shops in north Minneapolis. Sawdust covered the floor of each shop, catching the blood from the freshly-cut meat. These carcasses hung there in the cold, waiting to be chopped up. The butcher would cut up whatever parts of the cow we wanted. At the butcher shop we also bought whole kosher chickens. We used every part of the chicken-not one bit would go to waste.

I loved to go into the butcher shops with my dad and Uncle Jack on Sunday mornings to pick up our meat order for the week. It was the place to be on those mornings. People were always there gossiping, and the gumball machine stood at attention by the door, waiting for my pennies. Even the gum was at its freshest on Sundays.

A few blocks from the butcher was a kosher fish market, but it was not as exciting a place. We normally only went there to pick out fish for holiday meals. I remember seeing the fresh fish lying on ice with their wide, seemingly horror-filled eyes. They seemed to stare up at me, pleading to me not to eat them.

The kosher food markets were where you could first sense the growing excitement around the Jewish holidays. There were long lines at each counter, made up of the cooks from each family. Each was expecting the freshest fish for chopping into gefilte fish, or the leanest brisket, or the freshest chicken. I remember being in line with my mother and feeling the tension emanating from all the neighbors. The butcher was king at that time of year. He and he alone would decide which lady would get the leanest cut of meat or the largest chicken. The butcher addressed all the women respectfully by their last names-Mrs. Kreamer, Mrs. Goldberg, Mrs. Weinberg-no matter how many years they knew each other. Business was business. By the end of the day he was exhausted from serving all the yelling, demanding ladies of the neighborhood— each one wanting the best for their table.

In summer, we'd buy fresh fruits and vegetables from the back of a farmer's truck. He would come to our neighborhood every Monday morning. In the Fall we'd buy bags of potatoes and onions at the farmer's market on Glenwood Avenue. We always ate fresh salads complemented with an oil and salt dressing called boimyl in Yiddish. (My dad is still eating his salad every day with only boimyl on it.)

Our weekend meals were often eaten with members of our extended family. In the summers we would have glorious picnic breakfasts in a picnic area that felt like it was miles out in the country, though it was only off Highway 100. It had a wood-burning stone stove that my mother would cook pancakes on. (She made them from scratch, of course. She would bring her pots and pans and all the ingredients.) These breakfasts were usually on Sundays, and included my cousins, aunts and uncles, Grandma Tina, and Papa—at least fifteen people in all. My dad would bring a bat, a ball, and blankets to lie down on after our huge meal. My grandparents would bring folding chairs for themselves, which they would place under the huge trees. (By the way, this was where the famous Kreamer chocolate chip pancakes were invented. I was around seven years old when they were first served, and I have been making them ever since.)

This picnic area is still there, inside the cloverleaf that takes cars onto Minnetonka Boulevard from Highway 100. The whole area around the park has been built up, but the tables and brick stove are still standing as mementos of a slower era.

I went there recently to take pictures of this spot. Sadly, the tables and stove were covered over by weeds. But I could still hear all the laughter, and I could see my family, young and vibrant once again. Some played baseball; some lay sleeping on the blanket; others simply sat in their chairs, watching the kids play and hoping they wouldn't get hit in the head with a stray ball or flying bat.

Besides picnics, my most memorable meals away from home were at Aunt Betty's (not really my aunt, but a good friend of my parents in the neighborhood). When I would walk past Aunt Betty's house and smell her cabbage borscht cooking, I always knew I would be eating supper at her home that night. My mother never made cabbage borscht because she didn't like it. My good friend Linda, (Betty's daughter,) hated it, too but Aunt Betty loved it, and so did I. On nights when I didn't appear at my own family's table, my parents always knew where I was: at Aunt Betty's.

Me and Linda Israel Ellen (Aunt Betty's daughter) in Las Vegas in 1998 where she and her husband now reside.

I wasn't the only one who occasionally preferred some other mother's cooking. My friend Linda was wild about my mother's sandwiches. Aunt Betty would cut sandwiches into a couple of triangles, but Linda would watch in wonder as my mother cut her sandwiches straight up and down. To her, that made my mother's sandwiches truly special and it made my mother one fancy lady.

My mother was a fancy lady in a lot of ways. She loved to entertain on weekends, and I remember my parents throwing lots of dinner parties. They would serve anything from spaghetti to foods from the deep South, including turtle soup and jambalaya. On Sunday mornings my sister Bitsy and I would tip-toe into the kitchen for the cold leftovers. We would make this our breakfast while watching cartoons on TV before our parents woke up.

On my birthdays, my mom would make a surprise treat for the class and carry it the four blocks to my school. My birthday (in March) usually fell on the day of a huge snowstorm, but this did not deter my mom. The homemade cupcakes or cookies always arrived.

Back then, cod liver oil was the means for keeping us all healthy. Each day, before we could walk out the door, each of us had to consume that wonderful spoonful of yellow, thick, smelly, hard-to-swallow oil. We took it as if it were medicine. If some spilled down our clothing, the stain could never be removed.

In those days family doctors regularly made house calls. I still vividly recall the shots they gave us at home and the pills that came out of their black doctors' bags.

One other medical memory is going to the doctor's office down the block on my own when I was eight. The doctor was not my pediatrician, and my parents knew him but didn't completely trust him. One day I decided on my own that I needed to see him. I had a large lump under my arm and did not want to bother my parents with it.

In the office, the doctor looked at the growth and told me he could remove it if I would like. I said yes, and he gave me a shot of Novocaine, removed the growth, and bandaged me up. He told me I would be just fine, and he sent me home.

Dealing with my mother was another matter. When she saw the huge bandage under my arm, she got hysterical and immediately called my dad. She had him take me to my pediatrician and have him look over what had been done. It turned out that I was fine, and that the doctor down the street had done a good job but you can imagine the lawsuit that would ensue from this now. (I'd be a millionaire today!) But as long as I was fine, it never entered any-one's mind to sue.

Our dentist's office was just around the corner from our home, and I would go by myself when I was just six or seven. I remember having to have two teeth pulled, and my parents didn't even know about it until I got home with a mouthful of cotton, trying to smile with pride at having gone through it all by myself.

My mom made sure we three girls had all our artistic needs met—we had lessons in dance, piano, voice, art, anything imaginable. She saw to it that I took fencing lessons for awhile, too. She was a Brownie leader, taking her troop to Chicago for a weekend and, one year, being in charge of our Girl Scout cookie sale. I remember the dozens of cardboard boxes in the middle of our dining room much to my dad's displeasure.

As children, we always had pets, too. Bitsy would pick up stray cats, and we would hide them down in our basement, until Bitsy developed some strange skin disease she got from the animals. We also ran through many dogs of varied breeds. Soots, for example, I acquired at no charge one day. I was downtown with my friends, and a man was sitting on a corner with a box full of beautiful puppies. I bent down to see them and I was lost. He offered me one for no charge and told me it was not going to grow into a large animal-maybe the size of a cocker spaniel. I took him home and he grew into a Labrador Retriever—a huge dog who would jump up and ring the doorbell when he wanted to come into the house. He would sleep in the basement, and in the mornings he would jump in my bed, happy to see me. Sometimes he would jump so hard I would fall out of bed. Ultimately he went to a farm because my parents felt he was too big for our house and needed a place to run. They were right, of course, but I didn't think so at the time. I was heartbroken.

From there we downsized to a dog named Taffy. She was just a little bit of a thing, and she was (or course) the color of taffy. She lived a long, happy life, but was put to sleep after she began to sit in the middle of the street, not knowing where she was. It was a very sad moment in our lives, 16 years later.

As a child, the small town of Thief River Falls, Minnesota played a big part in my life. My Aunt Libby, my Uncle Milton, and my cousins Susan and Bobby lived there, and every summer our family would visit them. Thief River Falls is in the northwest corner of the state, only about an hour from the Canadian border. In those days it was an eight-hour drive from Minneapolis, on a two-lane high-way that wound through every little town. We'd usually arrive hot and tired.

But when we got there, it was worth it. We would play with our cousins Susan, two years younger than me, and Bobby, Bitsy's age. We'd swim in the Rum River, which ran through town, even when it was only about 65 degrees outside, which was about as warm as it got on some days in the summer.

Sometimes all of us would walk "uptown"-which to us big city kids meant downtown. In the drugstores we were able to buy a small sundae in a small Coke glass for two cents. It was one scoop of ice cream with chocolate sauce and peanuts on top. This was known lovingly as a Little Dick.

It was from my Aunt Libby that I learned the most about serv-ing, being a hostess, and enjoying fine things. Her husband, my Uncle Milt-my mom's brother-was the doctor in town. He had built his own clinic while also serving as the chief doctor for the railway company, and he and Libby were two of the wealthiest people I knew. I loved listening to them talk of their travels and worldly experiences. I remember having family dinners on her fine china and using her beautiful silver. I was always afraid that I would drop food on the imported linens covering her table.

Aunt Libby would take me shopping with her, and I would watch her choose home accessories with great care and put them in her home reverently. The bathroom towels were the softest I ever felt. Her manicured flower garden and lawn were cared for almost every day. She would regularly have beautiful cut flowers in the house. My aunt knew just what to do and say, how to entertain, and how to do anything correctly. She died without my ever being able to tell her how important she was in my life. I hope she knew without my telling her.

Much as I admired my aunt, after a few years she began to get upset over my arrival every summer, because I would bring with me my big city ideas. The small-town people felt that I would bring the ways of city kids to their children, and they were right. I was more outspoken than they were, and would talk about boys, parties, kissing, and everything else that I had experienced over the past year at school. I felt rather proud that I knew so much more than my aunt and uncle's kids did. In fact, I deliberately told stories that were designed to lift eyebrows. If I had had a boring school year, I would make up stories that would shock the kids, who of course loved listening to them. This continued until I had thoroughly embarrassed my aunt, uncle, Mom, and Dad—at which point I was ordered to behave. I then promptly closed my mouth.

When I was fourteen we went to Thief River Falls for what would be the last time before my uncle's death. On that trip, I tried playing golf with Susan at the nearby country club. On the beginning tee, I stood behind her as she came back with her swing. I was too close and got the club completely in my jaw on her backswing. This ended our game and landed me in the hospital. I didn't have a broken jaw, but I swelled up so badly that I couldn't open my mouth for days. I couldn't even get a finger inside my mouth to feel for any missing teeth. Susan felt horrible, but to this day I still wonder if she felt she got back at me for all the embarrassment I had caused her.

I didn't go back to Thief River Falls again until I was seventeen, for my uncle Milton's funeral in 1960. He died of a massive stroke in his living room at age 47, on a beautiful afternoon. My sister Bitsy was visiting them for the summer when it happened. He was in his living room, interviewing other doctors for his clinic, when he simply toppled off the couch, dying instantly. Bitsy walked in on this scene, which she will never forget. The doctors administered first aid and called an ambulance, but they did it only for my aunt's comfort. They knew he was dead, but they wanted an ambulance to take him out of there before she realized he was already gone.

My parents went to Thief River Falls for the funeral, leaving me at home-but when they arrived, my cousins asked for me. They called, booked me on a flight, and away I went on the first airplane I had ever flown in. It was a small prop plane that in 300 miles landed and took off three times in various small towns. The flight was a disaster. I vomited in the little bag and hated the whole trip. I drove back with my parents after the funeral.

A few months later, my cousins and aunt moved to Minneapolis, leaving Thief River Falls behind. I haven't visited the community since and it wasn't until almost ten years later that I stepped onto another plane.

<hr>

By the time I was twelve and beginning to attend junior high, I felt like a woman of the world. In junior high we had a choice: we could either bring our lunches to school or buy a complete meal in the lunchroom for 25 cents. After finding a worm, still squirming with life, in my chow mein one day, I chose to bring my lunch.

Each day I would bring two sandwiches (for I was a growing girl), a smelly kosher pickle, and potato chips. The sandwiches were filled with the same thing every day: very smelly liverwurst with Miracle Whip on white bread. I loved these sandwiches. My friends must have been very loyal, for they would sit next to me at lunch no matter how bad it smelled-or how bad I smelled after I'd eaten.

It was very different for a twelve-year-old than it is today. I had to wear a skirt and either a blouse or a sweater every day. Slacks or jeans for girls were strictly against school rules. There was no school bus service then, and we had to walk blocks to school no matter what the weather was like. On cold days we would freeze walking to school and back.

My first boyfriend arrived on the scene when I was twelve. His name was Chuck, and he lived across the street. Actually, he wasn't exactly a boy—he was eighteen. My parents would not allow me to see him or have him in our house. (Now that I have raised my own children, I don't blame them.) I disobeyed them, of course, and when my parents would leave the house, Chuck would visit. We would retreat to the kitchen for privacy and some serious kissing. Bitsy would always follow us—with her hand out. We would give her a nickel—sometimes a quarter—to leave the room for five minutes. Like clockwork, she would be back five minutes later for more money. (Bitsy made a lot of money when my parents left the house.)

There wasn't much to my relationship with Chuck. The only times I ever saw him were for those make-out sessions in the kitchen. Our romance didn't last very long, which was probably for the best.

* * *

In my thirteenth year we moved to a pink rambler on 8th and Upton Avenue North. It was brand new, like most of the houses on the block, and it had three bedrooms. It had only one bathroom, but it did have a garage—something we'd never had before. (When we lived in the duplex, my dad had to rent a neighbor's garage a few blocks away.) When we finally bought this single-family house with a one-car, detached garage, we felt like wealthy people.

Up until we moved, I had always shared a bedroom with Bitsy. Now, at last, I had my own room. I painted the walls pink, just like the outside of the house, and in the process covered the floor, windows, closet door and my whole body with paint as well. I never heard the end of that one, especially after I grew up and left home, and my sister Bitsy took over my pink bedroom.

I went to high school at the old North High, which at that time was at Broadway and Fremont, a good three miles away. (The school has since been torn down.) Most of the time I had to walk to school and back, though on many occasions my father drove me.

I lived at 815 Upton until I was 21, when I got married. Then my parents sold the house and bought another single-family home in St. Louis Park. My father still lives in that home. As for the pink rambler at 8th and Upton, it is still being lived in as well.

I went to my first big formal affair when I was only thirteen years old, sporting a big sty on my eye. I wore a rented formal, a beautiful soft blue billowy dress with a netted bottom and a strapless top. I accented the dress with a string of white pearls. My first corsage was a gardenia, which at the time I thought was a water lily.

The dance was at the Brookview Country Club, and my date was Marshall Shields, a gangly young man of fourteen or fifteen. Marshall's parents drove us there and picked us up, and I didn't know what to say to him in the car with his parents listening. It was quite awkward for us both—but I felt like I was on top of the world.

I was fortunate to have a mother who loved planning and throwing parties. For my sixteenth birthday, she put together a "sweet-sixteen" lunch. It was a delicious and splendidly served meal: creamed chicken over pastry, fresh fruit, and a big cake for dessert, all made from scratch. Each place setting had its own Coca-Cola mug filled with carnations.

As a teenager, all-girl social clubs were important to me. I belonged to B'nai Brith Girls (BBG) for three years. Our meetings were held in the Emanuel Cohen Center (its name was changed to the Minneapolis Jewish Community Center in the sixties). We met at the same time and in the same building as the boys' club, AZA (American Zionists Association). This is how we met our boyfriends and planned parties. We flirted and giggled while the boys strutted about in the halls.

My working years began as a baby sitter for the neighbors. I always charged a little less than other people, so I would be sure to get the jobs.

When I was sixteen, I got my first selling job in downtown Minneapolis in a small women's clothing store called Grayson's, on the corner of 8th and Nicollet. I earned 75 cents an hour plus commission. I worked evenings and weekends during the school year and full-time in the summer.

A troupe of dancers from Russia had come to Minneapolis to perform, and one day they all came walking into the shop. All were male, and not one spoke a word of English. I, of course, didn't know a word of Russian. All the men needed to buy women's girdles to wear under their costumes, to make them look slim.

At Grayson's, the dressing room was one big community room for everyone to change in. They all began trying on women's girdles, and I had to help them get into and out of these tight garments. They were totally mesmerized by the amount and variety of clothing we had. (Times were hard in Russia during the sixties.) I thought they would never leave the store. Somehow, though, we were able to communicate enough for them to get what they needed. That day taught me one of my best civics lessons—that the Russian people were not monsters to be feared, as we had been taught in school.

After Grayson's, I worked at a larger department store on the other side of 8th and Nicollet, the John W. Thomas Department

Store, which is no longer in existence. I sold toys, sometimes worked behind the candy counter, and wrapped gifts at holiday time. We offered free gift wrapping for men who made purchases over $5. Many men would give me two of the same item to wrap, but in two different sizes. One would be for their wife, the other one for their girlfriend. From nightgowns to furs, I wrapped two of everything much of the time. I learned a great deal about men at this job.

<hr />

My teenage years were also filled with finding out about my own sexuality and what it meant. When I was thirteen and completely respectful of all rabbis, a rabbi at an orthodox synagogue groped me. I ran, wondering how a man of God could do something like that. At that time, though, there was no one to talk to about it, and no place to go to get help. I've kept the incident a secret until now.

Something similar happened to me when I was a little older. I was riding home from work on a city bus. The man who had been standing

Graduation party for me, standing with Bitsy on left and Rachel

Close family friends—Dora Goldberg to my right, her daughter-in-law to her right, Dora's sister left side and Dora's son Norman behind us.

Sandy Winer's High School graduation cap and gown, June 1961

North High School before it was demolished and rebuilt in another area of North Minneapolis

next to my seat got off at the same stop I did. He got into his parked car, then followed me. He pulled up next to me, stopped his car, rolled down his window, and tried to talk me into getting in with him. I didn't, of course. I ran to a neighbor's house and called my mother. She walked over, and we walked back home together.

For me, the "north side" part of our family's story ends with Grandma Tina's death in 1969. By this time the rest of my family no longer lived on the familiar streets that were filled with the voices of my youth. We were now scattered throughout every suburb around the city.

Moving out of the city was considered the thing to do during the turbulent sixties. A different group of people had begun moving into the north side, causing fear and an exodus to the suburbs. There also began to be some anti-Semitism in the north side neighborhoods, plus racial issues and tension. Soon these escalated into physical fighting in the streets and schools. Eventually some Jewish-owned businesses on Plymouth Avenue were burned down. The shopkeepers left the city, fearing for their families' safety. Thus began the migration to the suburbs.

In the fall of 1997 I went back to my old Jewish neighborhood on the near-north side. I looked for the apple trees that I had climbed, sat in, and picked apples from. Sadly, they were all gone. But the homes, sidewalks, and schools were still there. They looked older, but not drastically different from when I was growing up. I took photos, some of which are a part of this book.

The Jews, of course, were long gone—having moved largely to south Minneapolis, or St. Louis Park, or other suburbs. Yet as I walked the streets once again, almost 33 years later, I felt as if I were thrown back in time.

Sandy Kreamer and Ed Winer

Ed Winer was born in St. Mary's Hospital in Minneapolis on November 7, 1943. His full birth name was Eddie Lewis Winer, though most people assume it's Edward. St. Mary's was a Catholic hospital—one of only two hospitals in Minneapolis that accepted Jewish patients and doctors at the time.

Eddie was the son of Edith and Norman Winer, who came to America from Russia in the early 1900s. They met in Philadelphia, where they were married, and after their first two daughters were born they moved to Minneapolis, where Ed and his younger sister were born.

Ed and I began dating at the end of ninth grade, and from then on we were inseparable. It was expected that we would marry once we graduated from North High School. We graduated at the same time and entered the University of Minnesota together. A year and a half later we became engaged.

Soon afterward I dropped out of college to work full-time and save money for our wedding and our life together. (In those days, it was considered more important for men to get college educations than women. In fact, it was widely assumed that women went to college mostly to get their "MRS" degrees) But even though I had left school, I wanted to be near my friends and continue to enjoy campus life. Therefore, I got a job in the University of Minnesota bookstore, which at that time was in the basement of Nicholson Hall.

As a member of Sigma Alpha Mu fraternity, Eddie took me to all his frat parties, some of which were truly wild. The frat house was old and going to be demolished, so there were no-holds-barred, riotous get-togethers. The frat once had a barnyard party, in which the guys created a pond in the living room of the frat house and filled it with live geese and ducks. At another party, they

Wedding Day—June 25, 1964

turned the stairs to the second floor into a waterfall. (As girls, we weren't allowed up those stairs to the second floor bedrooms.) There were always live bands, and beer was brought in and consumed by the gallon. After the parties we would go to Market Bar-B-Que to sober up and end the evening with barbecue beef sandwiches.

My wedding day left to right, front row: Grandma Tina, Bubby Ruby (Ann Dachis mom), Racheal Kreamer, Debbie Dachis, Elayne Kramer, Sheryl Riven, back row: Ed Winer, Les Riven, Rose Kreamer, Evelyn Riven, Ed Kreamer, Barry Riven, and Bitsy Kreamer.

With my mom and my dad

On November 22, 1963, President Kennedy was assassinated. I heard about it while working at the University of Minnesota bookstore. The whole world stood still in horror and sadness, and our lives felt totally out of our control. Our most revered head of state had been shot right before our eyes.

We watched and listened to every detail. Television cameras showed us the man who killed him. The future looked dark and grim.

Sometime later, again on television in full graphic detail, we watched Lee Harvey Oswald gunned down by a man named Jack Ruby.

A few years afterward, Reverend Martin Luther King, Jr. was assassinated. Not too much later, so was Senator Robert Kennedy, a candidate for president and the late president's brother.

These years were filled with social changes that altered the direction of the country. There were riots in the Southern states. Blacks sought the freedom to go to white schools, drink at the same drinking fountains as whites, and sit in a public bus wherever there was a seat—not just in the back. These racial fights escalated and spread across America. Newspapers were filled every day with the names of cities where rioting had taken place the day or the night before. Burnings and lynchings were common. Black churches were burnt to the ground, no matter how many people were worshipping in them at the time.

Eddie and I were engaged for well over two years before we were married. We chose a wedding day, I picked out a wedding dress, and we proceeded to make wedding plans. Then I found out that I was pregnant, and all the detailed plans went out the window. We decided we needed to get married as quickly as possible.

I was born in the era of secrets kept. Therefore, my pregnancy was a traumatic experience. When I found out I was pregnant, plans had to be made immediately. Abortions were illegal, and the furthest thing from my mind after seeing girls being sent away during school to keep the secret. How we handled this was through new secrets.

Eddie's brother-in-law, Irwin Riven, was about to go on a business trip to Sioux Falls (he was a traveling salesman), and we decided to go with him. Since South Dakota did not require blood tests before marriage or parental consent, it seemed to us the perfect choice. Eddie was underage at 20 years old, and I was 21.

With Eddie and I headed to Sioux Falls, South Dakota in my brother-in-law's car with my sister Bitsy and a blue dress, we were on our way. Approaching the Sioux falls courthouse, Bitsy and I jumped out of the car with dress in hand and ran to the nearest gas station to change into my blue wedding dress for my big moment.

Eddie and I got married while I laughed and cried with Bitsy at my side. After the ceremony, Ed placed a crackerjack box ring upon my finger and we were married. On June 18, 1964 we were legally married by a judge in the courthouse, with my sister Bitsy as a witness. The next day Eddie was back in school and I was back to work.

Looking back on it now, I remember being very frightened, which is why I reacted with both laughter and tears. While waiting for my brother-in-law to finish his day at work, our so-called honeymoon consisted of visiting the stockyards and having lunch in a chinese restaurant.

Before approaching my parents with the news of our elopement, we changed the wedding date on our marriage certificate—another secret we carried. Those social norms no longer exist, and were certainly shame-based. I was frightened and ashamed, but no other options were available. Two weeks later, after telling our parents, we were officially married in the home of my mother and father's closest friend. We had a religious ceremony performed by a rabbi. We spent our official honeymoon in a hotel in downtown Minneapolis, compliments of Grandma Tina. For 28 years we had two anniversary dates, still carrying that secret with us.

After Ed and I had been together for seven years, he was still an undergraduate at the University of Minnesota. We were very young and very poor.

It was at this time that I began my cooking career, trying to be as frugal as I could. I learned how to make a pound of hamburger last for more than one meal. Hamburger was 25 cents a pound, and $25 bought us groceries for a full week, provided we used a little creativity.

Eddie hated tuna, but when we had friends for dinner, I would make casseroles with it. I would drain and rinse the canned fish very well and tell Ed I had used chicken. He would eat it, enjoy it, and even compliment me on it. But if I were to open a can of tuna in the kitchen, he would not enter the room until the can was in the garbage and the table and counters were wiped clean of all evidence of the detested fish.

The social changes continued and the United States became a very unsettled country. The Vietnam War was raging. There was rioting in the streets and especially at the universities. No one wanted to go to Vietnam, halfway around the world, to fight in a war where we did not belong. Young Americans began fighting back, refusing to act like lemmings rushing into the sea. Free love was being preached. Mind-altering drugs came out of the woodwork, and soon they were easy for anyone to buy or grow. Flower children were everywhere.

Partly, the changes came about as a rebellion against the conventional lifestyle of the forties and fifties. Women stayed at home; men made the money and controlled everything, including all the members of their families. All of that was now coming undone, for better or for worse.

In the midst of all this, Ed and I were trying to make a future for ourselves, while wondering what was to become of the United States and the attitudes we were brought up with. In 1965, Ed graduated from the University of Minnesota and entered its law school; at the same time, he and I began raising our family.

Sandy Kreamer

The Winer Family

On January 30, 1965, Stephen Ira Winer was born. Stephen was the love of our lives and the savior of my soul while Eddie was in law school for three years.

This was a time of poverty for us. I did not want to work outside the house because I wanted to raise Stephen myself. Therefore I got licensed by Hennepin County to do child care at home. For a year I ran a child-care business to make money while Eddie studied. Then I worked at various jobs at home. I was able to raise my children without daycare while baby-sitting and selling Shaklee products. What a trick those years were! For supper we'd eat bread and butter, and vegetable soup from a can, and feel very noble. Those were the most difficult years of my life.

One summer we decided to become caretakers in an apartment building to make more money. We lasted only a few months. Cleaning out people's apartments after they had moved out was a horrid job.

During Eddie's last year in law school, we found a bigger, nicer apartment in St. Louis Park. It felt like a mansion to us. And ultimately our goal was reached. Ed finished law school in 1968, our debts got paid, and we began living.

By this time Stephen was three and I was pregnant with my second baby. With this new child on the way, we felt we needed a house for the family. Ed's

Contemplative Stephen, age 7

law school graduation was just months away, and he had a job on the horizon, so we ventured into the housing market. We found a home we liked in St. Louis Park just off Flagg Avenue on West 22nd Street. We were fortunate that my dad and Grandma Tina gave us money for the down payment.

When we moved in, I felt as if we were finally a real family, and my adult life was beginning at last. Each child had their own bedroom across the hall from ours. They were close enough to jump in bed with us—and also close enough for them to hear our quarrels at night.

Right after our move and only ten days before Lisa Michelle was born, I developed a blood clot and had to be hospitalized. My doctor told me that my condition was life threatening-not only for me, but for the baby I was carrying and for any baby I would carry in the future. Fortunately, Lisa Michelle was born without complications ten days later on May 22, 1968, only two weeks after we had moved into our house. But at age 26 my childbearing days were over; on my doctor's advice, I had a hysterectomy.

Lisa Michelle Winer Scholder at 3 years old

Although her birth had gone well, Lisa was born with a urinary tract defect that caused her to have one infection after another. It was very painful for her, and she only slept when I administered Phenobarbital to stop her pain. Then, exhausted from crying, she would fall asleep, only to wake up in anguish a few hours later.

During her first three years of life she was hospitalized many times. We scheduled surgery for her when she was at last strong enough to go through it. The odds were not in her favor: there was only a 2% chance that scar tissue would form valves where there had so far been none. But with the grace of God, the scar tissue did form, and we took her home, crying with gratitude and relief all the way. (Today, in 1998, Lisa is 29 years old. She is married, has a doctorate, and works as a psychologist.)

I had a cousin stationed as a physician in Hanoi, and we asked him to help us adopt a Vietnamese child. He promised he would try, but it took him two months of effort just to find out that the red tape made it almost impossible. With some sadness, we let go of that idea and went on with our lives.

Meanwhile, halfway across the world, the Vietnam War was raging. It was a very tumultuous, exciting time in history, a time filled with peace marches and rallies. I brought my kids to some of the rallies. Stephen loved to chant with me, "One two three four, we don't want your fuckin' war!" because then he was able to swear with everyone else. I would march with Lisa in her stroller and Stephen would sit on his dad's shoulders, carried high so he could see everything.

Actually, the primary reason Ed came was to protect us, because these rallies and marches often became violent. Emotions ran high- and even higher when you mixed in the mob mentality, drugs, and alcohol.

The Vietnam War wasn't the only reason people took to the streets in anger. I remember the days after Martin Luther King, Jr. was assassinated in 1968. Riots swept through Minneapolis and many other American cities. Outraged black people burned down parts of north Minneapolis, including parts of the neighborhood I had grown up in. I remember standing and watching the smoke rise. The smell of burning leaves from my childhood had become, just

15 years later, the smell of burning buildings. I stood and watched as some of the shops and homes that used to be part of my neighborhood, my home, my life-literally went up in smoke.

My little sister Rachel was a teenager during these chaotic times, and she was quite a handful for our parents. She was into everything forbidden-smoking, alcohol, drugs-and was very wild and uncontrollable.

The problems began when my parents moved to St. Louis Park just before Rachel entered junior high. She was at a very vulnerable age, and she did not know anyone in the neighborhood or at her new school. To be accepted by the kids who had grown up together, she had to prove herself. At the time, drugs were easy to find and inexpensive to purchase, and alcohol use was on the rise. For an adolescent trying to find her way in life, it was a recipe for serious problems.

Rachel teamed up with kids who liked to party, and things went downhill from there. Her school work suffered. So did her attendance. Often she would skip school and come over to our house instead. She felt it was her one safe haven. I never told anyone that she was staying with us because I was afraid she would find someplace far less safe to hide.

At that age, she was naive and gullible in many ways, and she had a knack for getting herself into unsafe situations-situations I would have to drag her out of. I felt that when she visited us we were harboring her for her own protection.

Rachel with dog named Taffey at 8 years old

Pre-teen Rachel Kreamer

Rachel Kreamer with her dog Phoebe in 1997

I felt strongly that the best thing I could do for my family was make sure they grew up healthy. We dug deep into the world of exercise and healthful eating. We had no junk foods, no pop. I served very little red meat, but I did serve millet balls, seaweed soup, and lots of laughs. My family never knew what they were going to have for dinner, and neither did our guests. My parents were afraid to have dinner with us. My kids were embarrassed by what I would serve their friends. The funny thing was, their friends still came to eat.

Juicing is what Lisa remembers most-particularly the sound of the swirling carrots, beets, and celery hitting the inside walls of the metal juicer. It spewed out this awful-colored juice-sometimes red, sometimes orange, sometimes green, depending on what went into the machine. (My kids hated coming into the kitchen in the mornings.)

Tofu was also a staple for us. I scrambled it, fried it with onions for breakfast, baked it in tofu lasagna-the recipes are endless. Often we ate it with brown rice.

I took many cooking classes, from Chinese to vegetarian to Indian. Over the years, this has helped me to be creative, and to look for unusual dishes that are healthy and delicious. When they were little, Stephen and Lisa were at my mercy-and they hated my cooking. Now though, as grown-ups, they are very careful about what they eat and make sure it's healthy. Even today, red meat is hardly ever on their plates. (Unfortunately, none of us could ever get rid of our craving for chocolate.)

Everyone in our family loved my homemade bread, which I served regularly. On our summer vacations, driving across the United States, we would take along loaves of homemade whole wheat (which weighed more than our suitcases), as well as a Tupperware container of chocolate chip bran muffins. When we did eat in restaurants, it was generally at good old truck stops, where portions were huge and food was served around the clock. We saw a great deal of the country this way.

But the most important meals of the year for us were (and continue to be) our Passover seders. Each year our whole family would gather: my mom and dad, Bitsy, and Rachel. For many years the seders were at my mom and dad's home; then, beginning in the 1980s, my home became the annual gathering spot.

I loved hiding the matzoh and watching the kids scramble to find it. My dad always came with a pocketful of silver dollars-one for each child. Other adults would distribute money to the kids, too, but they always went to my dad first for that shiny reward.

For me, Passover is a living symbol of religion, of family, and of the importance of sharing our heritage together. I have a great appreciation for my grandparents during this holiday.

My favorite room in the house doing what I love best

When we decided to try camping, I had to begin thinking a little more creatively about cooking. It wasn't easy figuring out how to feed my family in a tent trailer. From mountain climbing to snorkeling in the ocean, from Disneyland to Disney World, we experienced the United States dragging that trailer behind us.

The Winer trailer slept six, and had a stove, an oven, a little fridge, and a sink. The queen-size bed was for the parents, with an electric blanket we plugged in at night. Each child had their own bed. We didn't know how to build a campfire, so our electric wok became as necessary as our car jack. Stephen and Lisa always knew where our camper was at any campground. They would walk past other campsites, with their big, beautiful fires in their fire pits, smelling the aromas of hot dogs and hamburgers. But when they would begin to smell beef and broccoli in oyster sauce in the air, they immediately knew they were where they belonged.

Once we talked a group of friends into sharing camping trips with us. Five families made the journey together, and we became known as "Jewish Campers International." On one memorable trip through the mountains, the brakes on our car went out as we came down into Aspen on a horribly narrow winding mountain road. We gained momentum, traveling faster and faster, being shoved downward by the tent trailer we had been pulling. Finally, we were able to stop the car by steering it into a clump of trees, which stopped us from going over the edge of the mountain. But we had wedged ourselves between the two biggest trees and were unable to get out. We called on our CB for help, and the Aspen police rushed up to get us and take our vehicles into town for repair. (The up side of this was that we got a warm shower and a great night's sleep in a very nice hotel.)

On another occasion, I had to have emergency surgery for hemorrhoids in Estes Park, Colorado—a great place for hiking, but *only* if you don't have hemorrhoids. The only good that came from this was spending a few nights in a motel while our friends shivered in their tents in a campground on a mountain side. They slept tilting down the mountain; although I was in pain, at least I was in pain in a nice, soft bed on flat ground.

❧

Once my husband's law practice began to take off, I would have dinner parties for other attorneys and their spouses. I loved entertaining, often cooking and baking for days just to make one great meal. When out-of-town attorneys would visit, I would serve foods grown in Minnesota - wild rice dishes, cranberry salads, and the like. I've included the best of these dishes in this book.

For a few years, Ed and I belonged to the International Institute of Minnesota, which was devoted to helping people from different countries share their knowledge and experiences. We would be asked to pick up people at their hotel, take them to our home for a family dinner, and show them a little bit of everyday life in the United States. This was a wonderful people-to-people experience, and we hosted lawyers from all over the world. One evening we had attorneys from Egypt, Nigeria, Uganda, Jamaica, and Barbados—all at the same dinner! I felt as though I were at a meeting of the United Nations. The gentleman from Nigeria was a Muslim who was not allowed to eat meat or drink alcohol. Having him and an Egyptian man, also a Muslim, in our Jewish home made for a very interesting experience-particularly since the dinner took place in October, during the Jewish holiday of Sukkot. It is customary in some Jewish homes to erect a *sukkah* —a small, simple shelter with a thatched roof—to celebrate the Fall harvest. We had put one up, but it looked too much like the homes of many people in Nigeria or Egypt, so I had it taken down.

At another dinner we had a man from Portugal and a woman from East Germany. This was long before the Berlin Wall was torn down, and the woman was a serious Communist. Ed certainly let her know our leanings at the dinner table, much to my embarrassment. When she asked him what he did for a living, he told her he used to be an undercover agent for the CIA. I wanted to crawl under the table, but she did not appear ruffled. Still, after she had excused herself to go to the bathroom, I had this strange feeling that she would plant a bug somewhere. After the evening was over, we searched the house thoroughly, but found nothing.

When my kids were growing up, I felt that the more experiences I could expose them to, the happier adults they would become. Our family vacations outside the United States were chosen with that principle in mind.

On our first such vacation, we took Lisa and Stephen to the beautiful island of Jamaica. I found a hotel on the outskirts of Ocho Rios, an all-Jamaican town at that time. (Jamaica was and is, of course, part of the Third World.) We ate in the town and walked the streets at night. We were the only white people in the restaurants.

We would walk into town each day for groceries. Bare shelves lined walls where food for customers should have been. We saw kids with no shoes shopping along with their mothers. Beggars in the streets accosted us. It all made for a pretty grim picture of how most of the world lives.

Stephen felt horrible watching people in the grocery store. They would pick up food to buy, then later have to return some of it to the shelves for lack of money. He begged me to give money to the people to help them pay for what they needed. I told him that the people might be poor, but they did have pride, and I would not give them money as a handout when they didn't ask for it.

Because our hotel was so close to the town, the hotel manager had set up a program whereby the school children were allowed to come and swim in the pool during holiday vacations. Lisa soon became the only white face in a sea of little black school children.

Lisa had a lot of fun with the children until one little boy frightened her by telling her he loved her. She jumped out of the pool, ran to my side, and told me what he had said. I explained to her that he probably thought she was special because she looked different, and that she should just go ahead and play with all the kids. Back into the pool she jumped, and she continued to have a great time.

Everything my kids saw in Jamaica made an impression on them. When we were packing to leave, I noticed that they had left their tennis shoes and some of their clothing behind, so that they would be found by anyone who might need them. I was very proud of my kids for that. And with much pride in my heart, I watch them today as they continue caring and giving as adults. The spark of giving and sharing will never burn out. Please teach this lesson of life to you children.

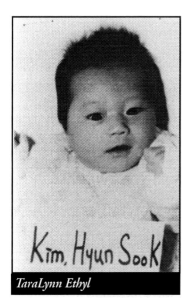

TaraLynn Ethyl

TaraLynn Ethel, my third child, was born in Seoul, South Korea on October 22, 1981. She came to us when she was only three months old, on February 14, 1982, but the wait for her felt like forever. Lisa was thirteen and Stephen seventeen at the time.

She was a beautiful baby, with big almond eyes and a lovely round face. When she smiled she would lose her eyes in her cheeks. She was flown to Chicago, where Lisa, Grandma Rose and I were waiting for her. We planned to catch the next flight back to Minneapolis, where the rest of our family was waiting for her in the airport. To our shock, she came off the flight very sick. Directly from customs we took a cab to the nearest hospital, where she became a patient for one week. She had pneumonia, just as I had as a small child. I stayed on with her and sent Lisa home with my mother.

Tara was put in an oxygen tent, which I would unzip and crawl in to be with her. I did not want her to feel alone in a new country with strange faces while lying sick in a hospital bed. I stayed with her from 7:00 a.m. until 10:00 p.m. every day. My cousin lived in Chicago, and I would retreat to her home in the evenings to rest and rewash my clothes, which I would have to wear again the next day.

We finally flew home together a week later. There was no fanfare at the airport—just our family to greet her and finally bring her home to her own crib, and into the loving, waiting arms of her dad, Stephen, and Lisa.

From then on Tara was beloved to everyone, especially her older siblings and their friends. The whole household treated her like gold.

<hr />

With Tara's arrival our trips became a little more limited, but they were exciting nonetheless. When she was four months old, we had her on the beach with us in Florida. Three months after that, Ed carried her on his back in a backpack in the Colorado Rockies.

Once Tara had joined our family, my resolve to always feed my family healthily broke down little by little. At first I was very careful, but as she grew up, I became lazy. She did drink pop and eat chips and lots of meat, but she seemed to thrive on this diet. By then, of course, we were both older, and I was tired of begging her to eat what I thought was best for her. She seems none the worse for the diet she chose.

It was quite an experience having three children of such varying ages. When we would go shopping, it always shocked me when I opened my purse. I would find a plastic paper diaper for one daughter and a sanitary napkin for the other. Such big age differences are not uncommon today, in 1998, but it was very unusual in those days. Back then we were on the cusp of societal change; today we'd be just a normal family.

My husband did not like animals, but I bought them for my kids anyway, thinking they needed the friendship and companionship of four-legged creatures. We had hamsters, turtles, cats, and dogs. Our hamsters always got loose in the basement, and we would throw food on the floor to catch them. Sometimes two would get loose, and when we put out food we'd find eight. They'd had babies down there.

Our turtles never lived long. When the last turtle we owned died, Stephen suggested that we put it in the mailbox for him to look at every day, so he could see what death meant. We did, but I alerted the mailman to what we were doing, and urged him not to look when he delivered the mail. (It was winter, so the turtle did not decompose or smell.) It took Stephen about three months of checking on his dead turtle every day to have enough reminders of mortality. Finally I was able to remove the turtle's frozen body for burial.

From there we went on to a stray cat that we found on our doorstep. Lisa was only four years old then, and she loved her new kitty. One day, though, I saw scratch marks all over her legs. Out the door the sweet cat went. (Only years later did I find out why the cat had scratched her: she and her friend would pick it up and throw in down the basement stairs, trying to find out if it was true that cats always land on their feet.)

Then we began with dogs. Our first was named Hot Dog. The kids were probably too young for a dog at that time, and we had a hard time training him. We found him a nice home, and no one cried over the loss. Then we moved on to Morris, a German Shepherd mix from the Humane Society. He loved the kids, and would run after the school bus when it picked them up in the morning. Often he would end up at school, going from one open room to another, looking for the kids with his tail wagging and his tongue licking anyone in his path. Eventually the message would come over the loudspeaker: "There is a dog in the library. If anyone knows who it belongs to, please come to the office." The kids would slink into the office and call me to come get him. I finally took Morris back to the Humane Society for someone else to love and chase after.

Fred was a mentally ill schnauzer/poodle mix who hated everyone except me and the kids. He would jump through screen doors to attack the paper boy or mailman, and he was feared by friends and neighbors alike. We took Fred with us on a trip to Canada, and lost him while we were camping in the Canadian Rockies. He wasn't heard from for ten days. We thought he was dead—perhaps killed and eaten by grizzlies—but to our shock he survived, and turned up very much intact. The Canadian police flew him back to Minnesota, first class, into my parents' waiting arms. (He wasn't able to bark for a few weeks afterward, probably from the shock of the experience.) We sent Fred to obedience school, but he failed the class when he bit a very experienced trainer. That was it for Fred, who we then shipped off to a farm.

The last dog we had as a family was a beautiful German Shepherd named Ariah. The kids and I loved him, but Ed hated him. Ariah knew Ed didn't like him and would go out of his way to make Ed miserable. He would jump on our bed and chew the mattress, only on Ed's side, until he had made huge holes in it. But Ariah loved me and would jog with me on the city streets, keeping up for five miles.

With Tara's arrival in 1982, I was afraid of what I'd heard some German Shepherds do when a new baby enters the home. (They get very jealous and competitive.) So, after four years of having a great buddy, I gave him away to a family who had other dogs and loved animals.

Today, in 1997, Tara and I live with two very sweet and cuddly cocker spaniels, Clive and Octavia. They are very sane, lovable dogs. Tara loves having them waiting for her when she comes home each day.

Our family trips, though less frequent, continued to provide us with some of our most memorable moments. When Tara was three, Stephen went to college in England for a semester, and I decided that the whole family should go visit him during his Spring break. After much planning, we packed up Lisa, Tara, our newly purchased backpacks, and flew to England. We joined up with Stephen and toured England together for a few days. Then we continued on to as many countries as Stephen had time to see. We only stayed in B&Bs, pushing Tara's stroller while we were walking and sightseeing. We traveled by train from country to country, ate a lot of fresh bread and hot chocolate for breakfast, and had a wonderful time.

Our first stop after England was Holland. We took a ship across the Channel, then boarded a train that took us to Amsterdam. We boated on the canals, visited many art museums, and ate wonderful fresh cheeses and fish.

After one such dinner, we strolled the streets for awhile, and suddenly found ourselves on a street where all the windows were lit with little Christmas bulbs. Surprised, we looked in some of the windows. To our amazement, in each one was a woman dressed only in her underwear, either dancing or lying around. We had unknowingly walked into Amsterdam's famous red light district. Our kids looked on with just as much embarrassment as we were feeling. The women in the windows must have also wondered about us with our kids, strolling the streets together. (Tara, in her stroller, was too young to understand.)

In Amsterdam we also walked through the same streets where, just a few decades earlier, the Nazi army had come through, pulling Jews from their homes and shooting them. I had seen quite a few documentaries about this sad time in history, but I was never able to understand the horror of it until I walked down those same cobblestone streets. I could hear the footsteps of the soldiers, guns in hand, running through those streets. Today the streets and their narrow rows of homes still stand as a legacy.

Also in Amsterdam, we toured Anne Frank's house, which is now a museum. It is a reminder of the horrors in the world and of what human beings can do to one another.

When she was small, Tara loved to eat grapes, and on our trip we would stop at fruit stores and outdoor stalls to get some for her. At one fruit and vegetable store in Amsterdam I began talking with the proprietor, who had a picture of several people hanging on the wall. I asked him if he had lived in Amsterdam during the war and who the people in the picture were. He explained that during the war, his parents hid Jewish people below this shop—right under the floor I was standing on. The picture was of some of the people his parents had saved—people he had known as friends and neighbors. He himself was not Jewish, he explained, but in Holland there were many sympathizers who tried to help their neighbors during the horrors of the war.

From Amsterdam, we took a train to Brugge, Belgium, and then down to Paris, where we stayed for five days. When we arrived, we found that our B&B had been overbooked and did not have room for us that night. The owner tried to find us another, but with no success. He suggested two options: sit up until morning in one of the many all-night outdoor cafes, or call a cab and stay in one of the nicest brothels in Paris. We chose the brothel.

I made the kids sleep with their socks on and told them not to touch anything, and above all not to answer the door if anyone knocked. But there were no problems. In fact, the owners treated us like kings and queens. They were delighted, because they did not have to change sheets every hour and we didn't bother anyone. They sent up hot chocolate and croissants to our rooms in the morning, and we agreed it was some of the best hot chocolate we had in all of Europe. Still, we ate and left as soon as we could, never looking up as we checked out.

We roamed the streets of Paris day and night. One rush hour, I took the family to the Arc de Triumph to sit and watch the traffic.

The crazy drivers would reach the arch from all sides, ending up in a giant circle of cars with no set rules.

Passover came while we were in Paris, and I felt the need to take the kids to a synagogue on Friday evening for Passover *shabbot*. I wanted my kids to be able to share something with other Jews in this part of the world.

We found the Jewish District and a synagogue. It was an Orthodox synagogue, one of the biggest in France. But when we arrived, something very strange happened. There were policemen surrounding the front of the building. We were frisked; all our packages from the shopping we had done were taken away; and we were moved along into the synagogue very quickly. The women were separated and escorted upstairs; the men stayed downstairs.

But then the service began, and in this beautiful, centuries-old, gold-filigree-filled synagogue we sang the same songs in the same Hebrew language as we did back in the States. Every synagogue suddenly felt like home, no matter where we were. In this foreign world we were exploring, we felt a sense of worldly togetherness.

After services, I thought it would be nice to talk to the people outside, shake hands, and wish them a good *shabbot*. But, much to my surprise, people grabbed their children and left immediately, without a nod to anyone. A cold shiver went through me. I felt the fear of these parents-the fear of the 1940s-and with my children held close, we retrieved our packages from the police and left as fast as the others.

Wanting matzoh, we walked around the corner to a deli I had noticed. This was the place we would have our seder dinner. But as we got to the door, we saw people being dropped off from their cars, then running into the restaurant and being locked inside for safety. When I asked a policeman what was happening, he explained that a few months before, the Jewish theaters in Paris had been bombed. That was the end of our seder plans.

The fear that came over me then was overwhelming. I suddenly knew the fear of being Jewish, but I also knew the importance of continuing our faith. The families living in Paris were not going to be stopped from practicing their religion. They needed to show their children bravery and continuity. Otherwise, millions of Jews around the world would have died for nothing. In Paris, my children learned this lesson by living in this fear along with me. They began to understand the importance of continuity and their responsibility as Jews. I could not have verbally explained what we saw and felt that night. This was one of the greatest gifts we could have received from God.

After Paris, Lisa left to go back home for school. We stayed on, touring the French chateaux and wine country, then traveled to Milan, Italy, and finally to Venice. For me, this was the highlight of our trip. We explored the streets and canals of one of the world's oldest cities-as well as the first ghetto for Jews, which was another lesson for us. We became friends with the daughter of our B&B's owner. She was a cute little girl of ten, and we took her sightseeing with us to the island of Murano, which contains the famous glassworks. We didn't get to see the glass blowers in action, but the beaches and cabanas lining the shore of the Adriatic Sea were spectacular.

My only regret about our entire European trip was that Tara was not yet old enough to feel and taste each country with all her senses. She did enjoy what she could, and I hope it has made a lasting imprint on her mind-even if she doesn't consciously remember the trip.

❦

Our last travel adventure together as a family was with Stephen and Tara in 1990. I wanted Tara to experience a rainforest before they are all destroyed, so off we traveled to Costa Rica. We hiked in the rainforests and drove into the Cloud Forest-literally a forest high in the mountains. We did not go as pampered tourists, but rented a truck and found our way around this small country by ourselves. We drove through villages that had cows and chickens running in the streets. We drove through the capital city, San Jose, which was protected by police with machine guns. We saw men who had worked all day in the fields walking barefoot along the side of the road, carrying machetes. We picked them up and drove them home, from one town to the next.

My kids learned a lot from this vacation, I think. Watching animals in their natural, God-given environments, not in zoos or pet shops, gave them the knowledge of how nature intended animals to live. The sights and sounds in the jungles showed them how the world had been before we began disrespecting and destroying it.

For the last part of our journey, we drove to a resort on the ocean for a few days' rest. There, after seeing Stephen off at 6:30 a.m. to catch a plane home, we felt something none of us had ever experienced before. Costa Rica was hit with an earthquake.

Our hotel was supposedly earthquake-proof, but you sure could have fooled me. Windows were shaking and rattling. The water pipes on the roof burst, pouring water into the hotel. (We were on the top floor.) I had never heard such a thunderous sound from the earth. I pulled a sleeping Tara from out of her bed, where the hanging lamp over her head was swaying, and held her close to my body until things quieted.

After the hotel had stopped shaking, Tara had to use the bathroom. While she was sitting in an uncompromising position, a second quake hit. I grabbed her off the toilet, held her close again, and prayed. Quickly, I dressed her in whatever clothes were nearest, grabbed her hand and led her, running, down the stairs. It was exactly like being in a disaster movie.

The stairs encircled the elevator shaft, and as we ran, we passed elevator doors which were open. Waterfalls poured down the shaft from the burst water pipes. On other levels, people were pounding on closed doors, checking to see if anyone had been caught inside. Fortunately, we made it outside safely.

Not so fortunately, our clothes were ruined from the water coming into our room through the ceiling. And, because of the constant aftershocks, staying in the hotel any longer was out of the question. I did not want to finish my vacation this way, so, with Tara wearing some of my clothes, we went to the airport and left for Florida.

It turned out that Stephen had just arrived at the airport when the earthquake struck, but the airport was not hit as hard and he was able to fly out as scheduled. But when he arrived in Florida to transfer to another plane, he had a minute to think about what he had just experienced, and he ran into the bathroom to vomit.

We were all worried about each other, which made for a few very frightening hours, until each of us learned that the others were fine.

A Changed Winer Family

In the spring and summer of 1992, I was busy planning Lisa's wedding. During those same months, I was living separately from Ed and trying to make sure all went well for my children.

But, despite my efforts, all did not go well. A few weeks before her wedding, Lisa's best friend and bridesmaid died in a hit and run accident in the Orient. She was on her way to the airport to come home for this happy occasion. She was dearly loved by all of us, and the tragedy of her death is still hard to think about. Happily, Lisa was married as planned on August 30, and the wedding did turn out beautifully.

I waited until this was done before tackling another trauma in my life. On September 2, 1992, just a few days after Lisa's wedding, I served Ed, my husband of 28 years, with divorce papers.

That year was quite a difficult one for us all. Until then I had been part of a family of six, including my future son-in-law. Suddenly I had a family of two: Tara and me. The two of us were in a relatively new home we had moved into a year earlier; it was quite large and hard for me to maintain alone. This meant my cooking days were over for the time being. Plus, the kitchen seemed huge and quite lonely, so Tara and I would have our small meals together in my bedroom.

Eventually I felt the best thing for us was to move into an apartment and start making a life for us there as best we could. We found a beautiful three-bedroom place with a balcony, a swimming pool, a party room, and all the amenities. We had just bought a puppy named Clive as a companion for Tara, and on August 1st, 1993 we moved into our new, smaller home.

A year later we moved again. Tara had been attending a private school, Breck, but we decided we would try public school instead. I did some research and learned that Edina had pretty good schools. So we moved to Edina-again to a three bedroom apartment. This one, though, was very large, so Tara could have her friends over, and so it would feel a little more like a house.

Finally, after another year, I purchased our current home, again in Edina. It is an old home, built in 1912, but remodeled extensively since then. I am in the process of converting it back to how it looked in 1912, which is quite a project. The house is in an old area of Edina, with large old trees, sidewalks heaved up from tree roots, and neighbors that visit one another. It has the same personality as the north Minneapolis neighborhood that I remember from my childhood.

One block away from our home is the Minneapolis city line, which means that Tara has her suburban school, and I have the city one block away. Lake Harriet is but a few blocks' walk from the house, through a lovely little shopping area called Linden Hills, which has a food co-op, bakery, yarn shop, garden shop, and wonderful little restaurants. The ice cream store with its shaded outdoor terrace is my favorite place to sit. Under its canopy of trees, I can people-watch or write on warm sunny days. It is a good place to start the day or to plan out what the day will hold for me.

My father loves to come visit, and we sit out on my front porch, watching the people and cars pass by, sharing memories.

The divorce process took three years, but in 1995 I at last became single again.

Since my separation, there have been many firsts for me to conquer. The most important one was the feeling that somehow I had failed. Born into an era-and a family-in which people did not divorce, I felt very ashamed. Women were supposed to keep the family and home together, and I hadn't. Our friends never knew how poorly our marriage had worked, and they were very surprised when we separated. Sometimes I felt as if I failed them as well.

It took me quite a few years to realize that I am me and can be me without being a part of we. It was a very hard adjustment, but I have finally made it.

I had to make adjustments financially, too. Before my separation, I had a lady to help me clean, a gardener helping me in the spring, someone to plow the snow in winter, and lawn service in summer. Suddenly, all of it was gone. I had to learn to handle money, investments, and all the bills. In other words, I had to grow up into the adult world.

But I've made it. I have survived-quite nicely, I might add- and I love being single. How long I will love this lifestyle, I cannot tell. But so far, its good.

Since my divorce I have begun charting my own course, exploring myself and my interests. I never really had the chance to do so before, and I do not want to stop. For instance, I love the pastries and sandwiches served during high tea, and have tried setting up a high tea catering service on a small scale. I soon realized, though, that this will take a lot of effort and money to start up properly. I will be watching for the right time and place for this goal to become a reality for me. Meanwhile, I still cook a great deal. I love doing it as much as ever, and now cook for my friends.

Over the years since my divorce, I have traveled to California to visit friends; taken a writing course in Taos, New Mexico; and taken my parents on a car trip to Mott, North Dakota, the town my mother was born and raised in, so she could revisit her past. I have driven down to Texas to visit Stephen with my friend Steve, and have travelled to Florida as well. I have many more places to explore; I feel as if I have only scratched the surface.

There is so much to learn and so little time. I have at last come into my own and am still evolving into who I am to be (that is, if one ever finishes that job).

Please, my children, never give yourself away so much that you never truly find who you are. And when you do find out who you are, never give that away, not ever...

Over the past few years I have grown close to my little sister Rachel once again. She continued her wild behavior well into her twenties and even her early thirties, but eventually she settled down. Only recently, in her late thirties, has she revealed why she was so wild. During her teenage years she suffered from child abuse-abuse which was kept completely secret. When this was finally exposed and the problem taken care of, she slowly began to recover. It took many years for her to heal, but she is now, at age 44, quite a woman. She is a successful travel agent, owns her own home, and has many friends.

Today, Rachel is back to calling me Sam, just as she and Bitsy did when we were younger. She is also trying very hard to have good relationships with my children. Last night she colored my hair for me-the first time she has ever done this. It felt very intimate, much like when I polished my Mom's nails for the final time a few months ago. I will be there for her now and always-just as I had tried to be nearly 30 years ago, and never knew why she wouldn't let me.

❦

I am now 54 years old and living with Tara, my 16 year old. I love her with all my heart, and will forever, but she has been a very hard teenager to raise. Soon enough her college years will be upon me, and I will then look for her in my silent house. The phones will not ring nearly as often. There will be no more going to sleep with the smell of popcorn and pizza wafting through the air.

I hate to give these things up forever. I hope my grandchildren will come to sleep at their grandma's house, and I can make them poppyseed cookies or bake bread with them.

Postscript

❦

After I read what I had written, I realized I did not touch on any interesting things I had done in my life.

I began to really dig into my life to find things that you would be interested in reading about, and yes indeed I did find a few experiences I had that was not shared yet. For one, I was a tom boy. It was safer for me that way. I found I could play with boys as well as girls and grew out of my shyness that way. Playing football during recess in grade school and basketball in junior high taught me I did not have to just stick to dance or just to sit in a corner and giggle with the rest of the girls. Those things had their place in my life,but I loved being a little more active than most girls were in the 1950's. As a teenager, I was quite rebellious and got into some trouble that my parents never knew about.

I smoked at a young age, often in the bathroom at Hebrew school after school. I remember once a teacher came into the bathroom when I was smoking and I immediately went into a stall and stood on top of the toilet so no one could see my feet if she looked under the stall while looking for the smoker. To my shock, I fell into the toilet because my foot slipped off the toilet seat and I found myself deep in the toilet on all accounts. Yes, I was caught. Also smoking in the synagogue bathrooms during the evening social girls club meetings with the rest of my friends. We almost lit the synagogue on fire. Luckily the bathroom was mostly metal, and there was nothing to burn but the toilet paper.

I did not start drinking until my college years, and then only at fraternity parties. Drugs were around but were not as readily available as they are now. While in school I never knew anyone who was using drugs. I was quite naive I learned. During my 20 year class reunion, I asked about drugs when we were kids and to my surprise, there were kids using them that I had spent time with and never knew of their use.

I never worked while married but my life was not wasted. Being a parent was very important to me and felt I needed to work in the community to help my kids and other kids like them. When Stephen was school age I had him tested and found him to be extremely gifted and talented. He needed another kind of education that the public schools weren't equipped to give him. At that time in my life Lisa was an infant, Ed had just graduated law school and we were paying back continuing medical bills for Lisa. The only option I saw for Stephen was for me to go to a private school with his test scores and ask him to be admitted, but on a scholarship. The headmaster told me I would not have a chance to get him enrolled. I literally begged him for the form to fill out just to try. Three days before public school began, a letter came in the mail telling us that yes, indeed, Stephen was admitted into Highcroft on a scholarship. We only had to pay half the tuition and I would drive him everyday to school because they could do nothing on the price of busing. Stephen was in private school for 2 ½ years. He learned a great deal and had a good start. In the meantime, I worked very hard within the school system where we were living, and the state department of education to form a chapter of the Minnesota Council for Gifted and Talented Youth. This was a very successful endeavor with the chapter still going on today, as I write this. They have merged with other schools and together now have programs in place throughout the year for talented youth. More should still be done today but it is progress and that comes very slowly in public schools. Through these years many kids have been encouraged by the programs I very proudly began.

In 1976 I began volunteering at the Jewish family and social services in Minneapolis. There was another wave of Jewish immigrants from Russia settling in Minneapolis.and help was needed for individual families assimilations. I was given a family, the David Rosenstein family consisting of mother, father, and two sons. I taught the boys English, took Alla grocery shopping and spent time showing them American life by incorporating them into our family.

Introducing them to my parents, we shared holidays as well. Stephen and Lisa learned a great deal of the culture they left behind from the stories they shared with us. My mother began talking to them about her cousin and her cousins family in Russia whom she never met but often heard about from another cousin living in California. My mother mentioned their last name, this was all she knew, and found them to be the Rosensteins neighbors when they lived in Odessa Russia. An amazing story.

In order for immigrants to come to America they needed a sponsor. Our job began as just that. The process took one year but we were able to get them out of Russia, and to Minneapolis to religious and political freedom they had never known. It was a very big adjustment for them, Celcia and Michael, along with their daughter Rya, and her husband Valerie along with Rya and Valaries' daughter and son-in-law Jacob. Three generations of our family I would have never known except for that little twist of fate. Rya was my mother's first cousin on her mother's side. These relatives settled in Minneapolis with our help and lived here for a little over five years, before moving to California. It was a beautiful experience for us to help get our family out of a communist country where antisemitism was rampant. They came also with a suitcase filled with stories of my cousins' deaths in Siberia from war, hunger and fear. Russian history was that of very hard living. Not living, surviving. No doctors care that was good, and food lines for whatever the government had to sell that particular day. And the employment was only where you were told to work or get educated for if you were lucky enough to fit into the schools quota of Jews.

They are living a much better, safer and healthier life now and I hope the generations to come will be told this story. Alona, Rya's

Fisrt cousins and sisters, first row, left to right: Celcia Starekova, Rose Kreamer; back row, left to right: Ethel Karson, Hatti Marofsky.

daughter has a son in college, Allen. One year after arrival to the U.S. Alona and Jacob had a son. First American born citizen, their families reason for leaving Russia—the promise of freedom for their children was met.

Jacob and Rya were very young when they married and are now divorced with Alona and Allen living in California, for future reference, Alona Vaysberg is a practicing attorney in Los Angeles. Jacob still lives in Minneapolis and has since remarried.

With the arrival of my third baby, TaraLynn, I realized that there were other Jewish families with children adopted from other countries of different nationalities. A support group would be needed for us and for the Jewish community to better understand the needs of these blended families along with their need for acceptance into the Jewish community. So I began a group in Minnesota called the "Stars of David". I had a great, wonderful circle of families that helped me to successfully carry it through for at least 3 years. When I was ready to give up my lead, for some reason, no one wanted to continue with the leadership. The group fell apart, people got busy with other things in their worlds and felt it wasn't necessary. During its heyday we had Jewish holiday parties together, held informational meetings bringing in psychologists to speak on issues of adopted kids and families. We also involved the Synagogues and heightened the awareness of the needs of these kids. Now as they matured into adolescence, the need for this group grew stronger but it no longer existed. This became a big regret in my life, that no one wanted to take over and continue with this group. I was getting calls from Jewish families in other states asking for help in starting their own Stars of David. I hope these groups are still in existence. I had made very good friendships during those years that I still enjoy.

It has been a wonderful time in my life with Tara, my youngest child whom I will cherish until the day I die. I felt her to be a gift given me to help nourish, love and protect while she blooms, like that perfect rose in my garden. God gave her to me as a gift, as all my children are, and they are all blooming in their own way, in their own time and I am there to water, and nourish them. Soon

Tara will leave my nest. The last of my baby birds will be on her own, and my life will have a different road to lead me down. That path is what I am beginning to look for now and where I want it to go. We seem to always have different times in our lives for different choices and it seems to be a great responsibility in being able to follow the right path in the right direction. It's very exciting if looked at positively. Changes are beautiful new beginnings. Please always remember this, changes are inevitable no matter how hard we may try to stop them.

My dating days with Eddie were filled with all kinds of youthful mischief. We would fill our days with each other as much as we could. When we were just beginning at ages 14 and 15 years old we would walk home from school together and do homework and begin to explore relationship boundaries, which were few. We experimented with our budding sexuality. During the summer months Eddie worked for his father in their plumbing shop, then he would come home and spend the rest of the time with me. When he finally got his drivers license we were free to spend our time at the "Clock" restaurant. The Clock was a great hangout for meeting all our friends 10-cent hamburgers 10-cent bag of french fries and a coke for 5 cents. We could get a meal for 25 cents. Today Mcdonald's can't beat the price.

On Saturday nights we would have enough money to drive downtown in Eddies first car, an M.G. sports car. We would go to the movies, have a B.B.Q. beef sandwich with fries and strawberry pop at the "Market B.B.Q.", then located on 6th Avenue near Glenwood. All this for $5.00. Oh yes, that was also when we would put gas in the car for .25 cents a gallon. Eddie was earning $6.00 an hour at his job and we could well afford an evening like this.

Knowing how I loved carmel apples, he would always bring me one in early dating years. Sounds sweet, yes? Well it was but there was also a sour side to our relationship. He was very possessive and jealous. I lost my friends and was not "allowed" to look at another boy. I thought this was because he loved me and I wanted a boyfriend who was on the football team and a wrestler, which he was. I thought he was quite a guy. Big mistake. After a seven-year relationship and 28 years of marriage I finally got it. I realized what I had done to my life, and wanted what life I had left to myself. I was just as much a part of this relationship as he. Unfortunately it took that long to see that I did not have to be part of it. Yes, I have three wonderful children from my marriage, and yes, some very nice memories of the good times, but the bad became a larger portion in my marriage and I knew this couldn't continue.

Traumatic as the divorce process was, the emotions dredged up within me were again based on shame. Divorce is very commonplace in the 1990s; nearly half of all marriages end this way. The fact that I grew up when no one ever divorced unless it was a life-threatening situation, made it especially difficult when I suddenly found myself needing to go my own separate way. The sense of failure in the role I was raised to perform was devastating. After 32 years with only one man, I was on my own.

It took many years to overcome my pre-taught values and inner rules. When I finally did, I felt as though I had been in jail for those past years and was suddenly freed. All the rules had changed, and it had taken time to relearn society's expectations. I felt as if I had been the only white elephant in a world full of beautiful gifts.

The three years it took for the divorce to be final were very hard years for Tara and myself. Stephen and Lisa were no longer living with us and were our adult children, but nonetheless it was just as painful for them as it was for Tara. It was the death of a dream for the entire family. Time passes, life goes on and we continue to grow and embrace what is given to us and make the best of what we have. I have learned to love what I have, not what I want.

I am now into writing, gardening, and continue to experiment with cooking. I have a wonderful man in my life and we are very

Steve Frieman

Ben Frieman

Deanna, Ben and Tara

Steve F. and Ed Kreamer

Deanna Frieman

happy. In a few years we can begin to travel extensively. Our kids will be independent since his children are Tara's age. Our responsibilities towards them will become less and less and more and more towards ourselves.

Steven Frieman is his name. He has been in my life now for six years. He has gone through a lot of bad moments in my life with me and for this I am forever grateful. He knows me better than anyone ever has and I know him. Sharing both our lives has been, and I hope, will continue to be the focus of my life now. Steve has his life activities and I have mine—which we both respect and love about each other. He is my best friend.

1998: The Menus and Memories Continue

We are now in the Passover season. My table seems to be shrinking, and the menu has become scantier, with fewer people to share the holidays with. Stephen lives out of town and was married last June. Lisa shares the holidays with her husband's family.

When the time comes, I hope grandchildren will fill my table again with laughter and light. Meanwhile, more and more, I feel the importance of having close friends as well as family to share festivals with.

Each year I look for something unusual to serve along with the basics my kids have known throughout their lives. Last year I prepared Chicken Tangine, a Moroccan dish that Jews in Africa eat during Passover. It's delicious, but a bit of a challenge to make.

I looked around the Passover table last year and saw my Grandma Sara in my mother's eyes. I saw my grandchildren in my children's eyes, and suddenly we were all eating the same meal, all sitting at the same table together.

Serving the hard-boiled eggs before dinner had a new significance for me that night. The egg is a symbol of life. Life goes around; it grows and continues, from one beginning to another, from my beginnings to yours.

I hope my grandchildren, and their children as well, will use the recipes they find in this book with as much joy as I had in using them and writing them down. Most come with some history. They each have something to say or a memory they carry with them that is part of you, through me.

I will continue to look for new recipes and tastes to share with friends and family. I hope to travel and discover foods from various regions of the country and world. I hope to share these at family dinners, as well as in another set of *A Menu of Memories.*

Each moment that passes will never come again. The memories and recipes in this book are my way of sharing some of the most precious moments in our family's past. These moments may be gone forever, but perhaps through this book they can be shared, relived, and passed on from generation to generation.

Family Memories and Menus Decade by Decade

Holiday Honey Cake
from Great Grandma Yenta

4 Eggs
½ c. Black Coffee—strong
1 c. Sugar
1 c. Honey
1 c. Oil
½ c. Raisins
½ c. Walnuts
½ teasp. Allspice
2 Oblong Pans or 1 13 x 9 in. Pan

½ teasp. Cloves
¾ teasp. Cinnamon
1½ teasp. Baking Powder
1 teasp. Baking Soda
3⅔ c. Flour
2 tablespoons Blackberry Brandy
Candied Fruit if desired

Grease and place wax paper in bottom of pan. Low oven—350 for 1 hour. Test for doneness before removing from oven.

This is the only recipe that is authentic from her hands I have to share with you.

Challagh

The following challah recipe was found in an old jewish cookbook and read pretty similiar to what my dad remembers when watching his mother bake bread on fridays. This recipe, or something close to it could have been made by my great grandpi moritz as well:

4½ teasp. Active Dry Yeast
   (about 2 packets)
1½ c. Warm Water,
   divided (105-115 degrees)
2 teasp. Salt
2 Large Eggs

⅓-½ c. Sugar or to taste
About 6 to 6½ c. White Bread
   Flour or All Purpose
   Unbleached White Flour
½ c. Softened Margarine or
   Vegetable Shortening

Glaze:
1 Egg Yolk beaten with 1 teasp. Water
Poppyseeds or Sesame Seeds (optional)

Mix the yeast with ½ c.of the water and 1 teasp. of the sugar. Let the mixture rest for 5 to 10 minutes, or until it begins to foam. Meanwhile, put about 4 c. of the flour into a large bowl with the remaining sugar, salt and shortening. Combine the ingredients until they form coarse crumbs.

Add the yeast mixture,the remaining 1 c. water and the eggs and beat the loose dough with a wooden spoon about 3 minutes. Slowly stir in just enough of the remaining flour to form a soft, slightly sticky dough. Cover with towel and let rest for about 5 minutes. Turn out the dough onto a lightly floured surface and knead it, adding small sprinkles of flour, if necessary, to keep from sticking for about 10 minutes, or until smooth and satiny.

Put dough into an oiled bowl and turn the dough so that all sides are oiled. Cover bowl loosely with a dish towel to keep the dough moist and dark. Let dough rise until doubled in bulk about 1 to 2 hours depending on the temperature of the room. Punch down the dough and knead a few times to remove any air bubbles. Divide the dough in half for two loaves. Then divide each half into 3, 4, 5, or 6 pieces depending on the number of strands desired for each loaf. Cover the dough pieces loosely and let rest for 10 minutes.

On slightly floured surface, roll out each dough piece into smooth strands and braid. Carefully set the loaves several inches apart on a very large greased baking sheet. Gently rub the surface of each loaf with a little oil to keep from drying out. Cover loaves and let rise until doubled in bulk,about 45 minutes to 1 hour or longer. Dough tends to stay in shape better if allowed to rise slowly at room temperature rather than a warm place.

Gently rub loaves with egg wash and sprinkle with poppy seeds. Bake loaves in preheated 375 degree oven for 40 to 45 minutes or until the crust is browned and the bottom of each loaf sounds hollow when tapped. Cool on wire racks.

Stephens Houston Texas Apartment; Stephen, Tara and Aunt Bitsy

Grandma Tina's Most Memorable Recipes

Poppyseed Cookies

Cream together:
1 c. butter
1½ c. Sugar
Add 3 Eggs
Juice of 1 Orange and ½ Lemon

Add:
½ c. Poppyseeds
4 c. Flour

Chill
Roll out and cut in circles with a drinking water glass
Bake 350 —10-15 min.
Makes about 60 cookies

Mamaliga

3 c. Boiling Water
1 c. Cold Water
1 c. Yellow Corn Meal

In a large saucepan bring 3 c. water to boil. Mix 1 c.cornmeal into
1 c. cold water while waiting for water to boil. Add to boiling water

stirring until thickens. Cover and cook on low heat about 5 minutes pour thickened mamaliga onto platter and dot with butter. Can be served with any kind of cheese on top. Cottage cheese is basically what grandma Tina used.

Eggplant

Cook eggplant directly on gas stove burner turning often while cooking until soft and skin is peeling off. Use low flame.
When soft and cooled, peel remaining skin from baked, soft eggplant. Cut the ends. Chop eggplant and add to it chopped green onions, tomatoes, cucumbers, radishes, green peppers.

Salt and garlic to taste

Pour into this mixture a little vinegar and oil. Refrigerate mixture a few hours before serving.

Great spread on bread or crackers. I would eat it plain. Definitely a favorite of mine.

Flanken:
known today as pot roast

Chuck Roast   Carrots
Potatoes   Onions

Little water in the bottom of the roasting pan. Garlic and salt to taste. Cover roasting pan, put in oven. Bake for several hours on low, 335 until meet falls apart

Chicken Soup

4 qts. Water	Salt to taste
Few Pieces of Stewing Chicken (and Eggs if found inside chicken left by the butcher)	Celery
	Carrots
	1 Parsley Root
Pair of Chicken Feet	Sprigs of Dill
2 Onions	Sprigs of Parsley

Clean chicken and chicken feet thoroughly. Combine with water and onion. Bring to low boil and cook on low flame 1½ hours skimming fat from top of water. Add remaining ingredients. Cover and cook on low again until vegetables and chicken are soft. Add more seasoning as desired. Best if eaten the day after cooking. The next day skim the fat off the top of the soup before warming, and enjoy. Great penicillin.

The Best Milk Coffee in the World:

Small amount of strong brewed coffee in a cup with over half of the cup filled with warm milk and lots of sugar.

Grandma Rose's Best Recipes

Lemon-apricot Jello Mold

4 small or 2 big
   packages Lemon Jello
2 Cans Apricots with juice
8 ozs. Cool Whip

Pour jello in 4 cups hot water and mix slightly. Chill for 2½ to 3 hours until slightly thickened. With mixer, mix into jello the cans of apricots with their juice. Fold in 8 ounces cool whip into mixture by hand. Pour mixture into oiled bundt pan and refrigerate until set or overnight. Unmold on serving plate just before serving.

Every holiday meal included this jello mold. It was one of the most requested food on her menu and she never let us down.

Sweet and Sour Meatballs

2 lbs. Hamburger
½ Bottle Ketchup
Brown Sugar
Little Lemon Juice

Roll hamburger into 1 inch balls and place in large saucepan. Add ketchup, brown sugar (according to the amount of sweetness you want), lemon juice (2 tablespoons) or to taste as it cooks. Cook slowly until done, maybe 1 hour depending on the amount made. Taste and add more ingredients if needed for flavor.

Easy dish used as an appetizer for the holidays. I use this recipe at other times because people love these over white rice as an entree. Dipping challah bread into this delicious sauce is a real treat.

Beans and Short Ribs

Drained cans of Butter Beans
3 lbs. Short Ribs

Same recipe for sauce as sweet and sour meatballs only larger amounts.

Put all together in casserole, cover and bake in oven basting often with juice from melted sugar ketchup and lemon juice on the bottom of casserole. Bake 1 ½ hours on 325-350 degrees.

The meat falls off the bones and we love to suck the juice off the bare bones.

Traditional Meatloaf

2 lbs. Hamburger
2 Eggs Beaten
Little Worcestershire Sauce
1½ teasp. Salt

1 teasp. Garlic Salt
1 teasp. Minced Onion
¼ c. Ketchup
1 c. Rolled Oats

In large bowl combine all ingredients and mix well. Pat into 9 x 5 loaf pan. Bake in preheated oven 350 degrees for 1 hour. Spread ketchup on top of cooked loaf and continue baking 15-20 minutes longer. Unmold and serve with mashed potatoes, one of my favorites growing up at home.

Hot Fruit Compote

1 package Vanilla Wafers Cookies
2 cans Fruit for Salad, drained
2 cans drained pitted Black Cherries
1 can Applesauce
3 tablespoons Brandy

Drain fruit and place in refrigerator overnight. Drain again in colindar and arrange in casserole over 1 package crushed vanilla wafers. Add little brown sugar if desired and lemon juice. Place in 350 degrees oven for 1 hour uncovered.

One of Tara's favorite dishes which my mom would never forget to make for her.

Salmon Patties

1 can salmon drained and bones and skin removed
1 Egg
1 Minced Onion
Garlic Salt to taste

Mix all together. Form patties as you would hamburger patties and cook in fry pan sprayed with oil until cooked through.

Rice pilaf

¼ lb. Butter
2 c. Rice, white, not instant
1 can Consomme Soup
1 can Onion Soup
2 cans Water

2 c. Noodles (optional)
Slivered Almonds
Mushrooms
Brown Rice in Butter

Add rest of ingredients and cook covered over low heat until liquid has absorbed.

Always a delicious side dish served with brisket roast.

Peach Kugel

1 pkg. wide Noodles—cooked
1 c. Peach Juice
8 oz. Cottage Juice
1 pt. Sour Cream

1 stick melted Butter
4 Eggs
1 c. Sugar

Mix all ingredients with mixer until well blended. Add to cooked noodles pour into greased 9 x 13 pan. Bake 350 degrees 1 to 1½ hours.

This recipe is so good I had to pass it out to friends and extended family members. I couldn't keep this one secret.

Sour Cream Coffee Cake

½ c Shortening
1 c. Sugar
2 Eggs
1 T. Baking Powder

1 teasp. Vanilla
1 teasp. Baking Soda
2 c. Flour
1 c. Sour Cream

Filling:
1 T. Butter
⅓ c. Sugar
2 teasp. Cinnamon

Cream eggs, shortening and sugar. Add the other ingredients and mix. Place ½ of the batter in a greased 9 x 9 bread loaf pan. Sprinkle ½ filling over first half. Top with remaining batter and sprinkle top with rest of the filling. Bake 350 degrees 30 to 35 minutes.

Banana Cake

2 c. Cake Flour
1 teasp. Baking Powder
1 teasp. Baking Soda
1⅓ c. Sugar
½ c. Spry

1 c. mashed Bananas
1 teasp. Vanilla
2 Eggs
½ c. Sour Milk

Mix liquid ingredients all but soured milk. Add mashed bananas. To sour milk, add 2 tablespoons vinegar to milk and let sit 10 to 15 minutes. Add dry ingredients alternately with the sour milk and mix 3 minutes of high speed. Pour in greased 9 x 13 pan.
bake 30-35 minutes at 350 degrees.

Best when using old (over-ripe) bananas.

Fudge Frosting for Banana Cake

1 c. Sugar
1 square Baking Chocolate
⅓ c. Milk

¼ c. Spry
1 teaspoon Vanilla
Chopped Walnuts (optional)

Boil all but vanilla on low flame stirring constantly. Let boil 1 minute. Remove from stove and add vanilla and nuts while stirring constantly until mixture hardens. Pour over cool cake.

Pecan Pie

3 Eggs beaten
1 c. Dark Karo Syrup
½ teaspoon Salt

1 c. Sugar
1 teasp. Vanilla
⅔ c. Pecans

Mix all together and pour into uncooked pie shell.

Bake 450 degrees-10 minutes. Bake 350 degrees 30 minutes take out immediately and let cool completely before serving.

Sandy Kreamer Winer's Family Favorites and Other Assorted Goodies

Chicken Wings

1-12 oz. Chili Sauce
1-10 oz, Grape Jelly
2 T. Lemon Juice
Garlic Powder

16 oz. Sweet & Sour Sauce
7⅛ oz. jar Junior Baby Foods
   Peaches
¼ teasp. Powdered Ginger

Line roasting pan or cookie sheet with foil. Place chicken wings on pan. Boil all ingredients until jelly melts. Place ¾ sauce over chicken and bake 1½-2 hours basting and turning often. Brush with reserve sauce and bake another 20-30 minutes. Bake 350 degrees.

Chinese Chicken Wings

Blend 1 c. Water
1 c. Soy Sauce
1 c. Brown Sugar or White Sugar
¼ c. Pineapple Juice
¾ c. Oil

1 teasp. Ginger
1 teasp. Garlic Powder
4 chopped Garlic Cloves
1 T. Lemon Juice

Blend all ingredients in blender. Pour over chicken wings and marinade overnight. Bake in oven 350 degrees for 1 hour.

Roasted Pepper and Artichoke Tapenade

1-7 oz. Jar Roasted Red
Bell Peppers, drained
1-6 oz. Jar Marinated
Artichokes, drained
½ c, minced Chopped Parsley

½ c. Parmesan Cheese
⅓ c. Olive Oil
¼ c. drained Capers
4 Garlic Cloves Chopped
1 T. Lemon Juice

Process all together and refrigerate before serving with crackers or pita cut into quarters.

Mon Doo
(Korean Eggroll)

1-package Coleslaw Mix
1 lb. Ground Chicken Meat

½ lb. Baby Shrimp

Seasoning Ingredients:

2 T. Sesame Oil
2 T. Soy Sauce
2 T. Rice Wine

3 T. Corn Starch
2 chopped Green Onions
Salt and Pepper to taste

Dipping Sauce:

2 T. Apricot preserves
1 teasp. Vinegar

1 T. Rice wine

Fry meat and add cabbage and seasoning ingredients. Wrap spoonful of meat mixture in wonton wrappers and fry in hot oil until browned. Remove with slotted spoon and place in paper towel to drain. Serve with dipping sauce.

Sandy's version of Korean man doo. Tara loved making this with me. We would take the ingredients and my electric frying pan into her classroom during her elementary school years and make this recipe for the kids in her classroom honoring her arrival date.

Barbecue Spare Ribs

2½ lbs. Spareribs
1 c. Soy Sauce
½ c. Pineapple Juice

¼ c. Dry Sherry
1½ T. Light Brown Sugar
4 cloves peeled, crushed garlic

Cut ribs into 2" sections and place into a large bowl. Combine remaining ingredients and mix into ribs to marinade 6 hours at room temperature. Turn often. Broil, turning often for 15 minutes on each side, basting often. Place ribs in oven at 350 degrees, basting again with marinade and allow to finish cooking. About another 20-30 minutes.

This is a real crowd pleaser.

Seafood Dip

2 pkgs.(8 oz.) Cream Cheese
1 pkg.(8 oz.) Imitation
    Crab Delight Flakes
2 T. finely chopped Onion
1 T. Horseradish

1 teasp. Worcestershire Sauce
4-5 drops Hot Pepper Sauce
¼ c. finely Chopped Walnuts
Paprika

Stir softened cream cheese. Blend in remaining ingredients except walnuts and paprika. Bake uncovered in 9 in. pan topped with walnuts and paprika uncovered . Bake in 375 degree oven for 25 minutes, or until lightly browned.

Roll Appetizers

1-8 oz. softened Cream Cheese
4 ozs. Sour Cream
1 c. shredded Cheddar Cheese
4 oz. chopped Black Olives

1-4 oz.can chopped Green Chili
  Peppers (mild)
½ c. chopped Green Onions
Add a little Garlic Powder

Stir ingredients together and spread on a 10 inch flour tortilla. Roll up and wrap in saran wrap. Place in refrigerator or freezer overnight. Slice pieces on the round and toothpick each piece for serving.

Babba Ganouch

Eggplant (large)
½ c. Plain Yogurt
2 Cloves Garlic

1 teasp. Salt
Juice of a Small Lime

Cook eggplant 400 degree oven for 20 minutes or until soft. Peel and blend with ½ c. yogurt, garlic., salt and lime. Puree in blender. Spread on plate and top with olive oil and dress with cilantro or parsley.

Strawberry Soup

15 ozs. Frozen Strawberries
 with juice thawed
15 oz. Sour Lean Sour Cream
1 oz. (1 tsp.) Vanilla

3 oz. Powdered Sugar
12 oz. Grenadine Syrup
2 oz. Half and Half

Mix strawberries and sour lean until well blended. Mix rest of ingredients but half and half. Blend half and half last. Chill and before serving place a fresh strawberry in each bowl.

Cream of Banana Soup

1.5 gallon Banana Ice Cream
1 .5 gallon Milk
2 oz. Myers Dark Rum

6 Bananas
1 Mint Leaf

Place ice cream, bananas and rum in a blender and cream. Serve in cups, garnishing with mint leaf.

Peach Yogurt Soup

1 bag Frozen Sliced Peaches
2 c. Orange Juice
2 T. Honey

1 carton (16 oz) Vanilla Low Fat
   Yogurt
1 c. Frozen(or fresh) Blueberries

Pour half ingredients except blueberries and yogurt into a blender
and blend on high until peaches are smooth, pureed. Add yogurt
until just blended.

Serve, adding blueberries on top in individual bowl.

Carrot Soup

2 lb. Package of Carrots
1 c. Chicken Broth
1 c. Vegetable Broth
Cayenne Pepper to taste

1 Onion
Garlic, as much as you like to
   cook with
½ c. Cream or 1 c. Milk

Boil carrots until soft in water and chicken broth. Save broth and
blend carrots with chicken broth in blender. Add remaining ingredients. Fry onions and garlic before blending them into to soup.
Add cream and taste, adding more seasoning as desired. Pour back
in pan and cook until hot, not boiling. Serve.

Yellow Pea Soup

Olive oil (2t.)	¼ teasp. Cardamom
2 chopped Onions	1 T. Soy Sauce
sauteed in a pan	Water
2 pinches Cayenne Pepper	Split Yellow Peas
2 teasp. Cumin	Crushed Garlic Cloves(3)
½ teasp. Cinnamon	1 large Vegetable Cube

Saute seasons, onions and soy sauce in the olive oil. In water, just to cover, cook yellow peas until water is absorbed , adding water until peas are mushy, at least 1 hour. Put all ingredients together, mix well. Squeeze lemon juice on top before serving after heating.

Great to give to people who have the flu.

Bean and Barley Soup

1 package Manishcevitz Dry	Onion
Vegetable or Barley	½-¾ c. quick cooking Barley
Soup package	Soup Meat
Carrots	Lawreys Seasoning Salt

In large pan of water, cook onion and meat on low flame, skimming fat off the top of the water from the cooking meat. After 1 hour, add soup package, and rest of ingredients plus any other vegetables you like. Add seasoning and cook slowly, tasting every so often. Tastes better a day after but you have to add water because soup thickens because of the added barley.

Layered Fruit Compote

2 c. Milk
1 (8 oz) carton Plain Yogurt
1 (3½ oz) pkg. Instant Vanilla
   pudding mix
½ teasp. Vanilla
½ teasp, Almond extract
4 (17 oz.) cans Apricot
   halves, drained

1(20 oz.) cans Pineapple
   Chunks, drained
1½ lbs. seedless Green Grapes,
   halved (4 cups)
1½ lbs. seedless Red Grapes (4
   cups)
2 Kiwi, peeled, sliced

Combine milk, yogurt, pudding mix and extracts in mixing bowl
and beat until blended. Cover bowl and place in refrigerator until
serving. Cut apricot halves and layer in a 5 qt. glass bowl with rest
of fruit. Spoon dressing over fruit when served.

Hot Fruit Compote

4 Grannysmith Apples
2 T. Lemon Juice

1-16 oz. Pineapple Chunks
1 bag Frozen Strawberries

Peel and slice apples. Line bottom of 13 x 9 pan with the apples.
Sprinkle lemon juice on top. Add pineapple and strawberries.
Mix ½ c. flour, ¾ c. Brown sugar and ⅓ c. soft margarine with 1 c.
oatmeal and ½ teasp.cinnamon. Sprinkle this on top of fruit and
bake in 350 degree oven for 1 hour. Let set for 15 minutes before
serving.

Brown Rice Salad

1 cup Brown Rice, cooked
1 Tomato-cut up
1 Cucumber, cut up
Parsley, Salt and Pepper to taste
Pour on Italian Dressing after all mixed together
Refrigerate overnight and serve

Chinese Chicken Salad

4 c. Vegetable Oil
½ c package Rice-Stick Noodles

Marinade:

2 T. Soy Sauce
1 T. Dark Oriental
   style Sesame Oil

2 Whole Chicken Breasts
   boned, skinned and sliced
2T. Vegetable Oil

Dressing:

½ Clove Garlic
1 T. Sugar
1½ teasp. Dry Mustard
1 T. Peanut Butter
1 T. Sesame Oil

¼ teasp. White Pepper
1½ T. Vinegar
2T. Soy Sauce
½ c. Chicken; stock
½ c. Vegetable Oil

Garnishes:
Cut up lettuce, onions, red bell pepper, sesame seeds

Heat oil and cook noodles ⅓ at a time. Marinade chicken covered in refrigerator 2 hours to overnight. Heat remaining 2 T. of oil and saute chicken. Cool, shred and dice, saving pan juices. Make dressing in a blender until all combined. While machine is running, add a thin stream of oil until well blended—set aside. Make salad—noodles on the bottom, lettuce next, chicken, onion, cilantro, peppers and sesame seeds. Serve cold. Serves 6.

Chicken Couscous Salad

3 Whole Chicken Breasts
  skinned and halved
1-10 oz, box Quick Cooking
  Couscous
2-14½ oz. cans Chicken Broth
1 Tomato, chopped

3 Green Onions, chopped
¾ c. drained canned Chick-Peas
  (Garbanzo Beans)
½ Red Bell Pepper sliced
½ c. Dried Currants
¼ chopped fresh Parsley

Dressing:
6 T. Fresh Lemon Juice
6 T. Olive Oil
¼ teasp. Ground Cumin
¼ teasp. Curry Powder

1 drop Hot Pepper Sauce
Pinch of Garlic Powder,
  Salt and Pepper to taste
⅓ c. Toasted Pine Nuts

Combine chicken and broth in a large skillet. Simmer until chicken is tender, remove and save the broth. Bone chicken and shred, transfer to large bowl. Bring broth to boil and add couscous. Mix thoroughly with fork and bring to boiling. Cover, remove from heat and let stand for broth to absorb. Cool and transfer to bowl with the chicken. Add to chicken the tomato, green onions, chic-peas, bell pepper, currants and chopped parsley. Mix well until combined.

Dressing: blend dressing and add to couscous and refrigerate at least 1 hour. Before serving top with pine nuts.

Turkey and Pasta Salad

1-16 oz. pkg. dry Radiatore Pasta
1 pkg. 8 oz. Pea Pods
2 lbs. Deli Roast Turkey cut
   (6 cups)
1 c. Celery (3 ribs)
1 Bunch Green Onions

2-(12 oz), cartons Byerly's Dill Dip
   or any other purchased dill dip
2 T. Lemon Juice
½ teasp. Black Pepper
Garnish with Dill Springs

Cook pasta. Cool. Add all ingredients and mix well. Refrigerate until cold. Top with dill sprigs and serve.

Easy Chicken or Turkey Salad

Prepared Chicken White
   Meat or Turkey Meat
½ c. Sour Cream
½ c. Mayonnaise
Cooked tiny Pasta Shells
   or Circles

Celery cut up
Garlic Powder
Salt and Pepper to taste
Cut up Red and Green Grapes

After cooking pasta and cooling it, add rest of ingredients and refrigerate before serving in a bowl lined with lettuce.

Turkey-Wild Rice Supreme

1 c. Wild Rice
4 c. Water
Cook to boiling and simmer
  covered 45-55 min.
1 carton Mushrooms
¼ c. Butter
6 T. Flour

1 c. Water
1 can Evaporated Milk
3-4 c. Cooked Turkey
12 oz. Jar Pimentos
1 can Water Chestnuts drained
½ Sliced Almonds
1 Bullion Cube

Saute mushrooms in butter. Stir in flour and bullion cube. Slowly
stir in water, and evaporated milk and cook until thickened, add
rice and a little salt and garlic to taste. Add turkey, pimentos and
chestnuts. Pour into greased 9 x 13 pan. Sprinkle top with almonds
and bake 350 degrees ½ hour covered and ½ hour uncovered.

Mexican Casserole

Corn Tortillas pkg.
Shredded Cheese
Small can diced Green Chilies

Green and Black Olives
2 Eggs
Buttermilk

Rip tortillas and place in 9 x 13 pan. Layer shredded cheese, can
diced green chilies, green and black olives. Whip eggs and buttermilk and pour over casserole. Bake 35 minutes in 350 degree oven.

Black Beans and Corn Salad

Can Black Beans
1 pkg. Frozen Corn
1 can cooked Corn
Minced Red Bell Pepper
Tortilla Chips
Dressing
Garlic

Salt
Crushed Red Pepper
Black Pepper
Lime Juice-touch
Olive Oil
Fresh Parsley and Cilantro

Drain can of beans. Add corn to beans fry in olive oil quickly the tortilla chips if you would like. Add diced purple onions. Add dressing and serve.

Mom's Great Chili

Little Red Wine Vinegar

1½ lbs. Ground chicken
1 can Chili Tomatoes diced
   with Chili Spices
1-8 oz. Tomato Sauce

1 pkg. Mild Chili Seasoning
1 can Red Kidney Beans
Little Red Wine Vinegar

Fry ground chicken in little olive oil and drain well. Place in pan and add rest of ingredients. Simmer slowly about ½ hour before serving. Serve with crackers, shredded cheese, green onions and sour cream to add to chili.

Salmon Puff

1 lb. Can Calmon	½ teasp. Dry Mustard
4 T. Butter	½ teasp. Worcestershire Sauce
3 T. Flour	1 c. Milk
1 tsp. Salt	4 Eggs separated

In a saucepan melt butter. Stir in flour, salt, mustard and Worcestershire sauce until blended. Slowly stir in milk and cook stirring constantly until thick. Cool 10 minutes. Beat egg yolks one at a time in a medium bowl. Beat egg whites until stiff and fold into yolks and flaked salmon, (do not drain salmon), Pour into 2½ qt. casserole. Bake 40-45 minutes at 375 degrees until its puffy and golden. Serve at once.

Jambalaya
-serves 8

1 oz. Canadian Bacon	¾ teasp. Thyme
1 l6. Smoked Turkey Sausage	1 Bay leaf
1 c. Chopped Onion	½ teasp. Tabasco or to taste
1 c. Chopped Green Pepper	½ teasp. Ground Pepper
1 T. Garlic	¾ c. Rice
3 c. chopped Fresh Plum Tomatoes	1 lb. Sea Scallops
1 c. Chicken Broth	2⅔ lbs. Jumbo Shrimp
2 c. Turkey Ham	½ c. finely chopped Italian Parsley
1 c. Tomato Juice	

Saute turkey, sausage, onion, green pepper and garlic. Add tomatoes, broth, juice, thyme, bay leaf, tabasco and pepper and cook 10 minutes. Stir in rice and cover for 15 minutes. Add fish, cover and place in oven at 350 degrees for 30 minutes. Transfer to serving platter and garnish with parsley, discard bay leaf and serve.

Baked Beans and Turkey Sausage

6-8 cans drained variety canned Beans, i.e. Butter Beans, Kidney Beans, Navy Beans, etc	¾ c. Brown Sugar
	½ c. Yellow Mustard
	1c. Ketchup
	1 T. Worcestershire Sauce
2 medium chopped Onions	½ c. Barbeque Sauce

Place all in a crock-pot and simmer on low all day or at least 8 hours.

Chicken Breasts with Wild Rice

1 c. Wild Rice	1-4 oz. Undrained Mushrooms
4 c. Water	¼ c. Dry Sherry
1 can Cream of Mushroom Soup	6 boneless Chicken Breasts
1-8 oz. Sour Cream	½ c. Parmesan Cheese

Buttered 9 x 13 pan. Place cooked wild rice on bottom. Place chicken breasts on top of rice. Pour over mixed wet ingredients. Sprinkle parmesan cheese on top of sauce and bake 375 degrees 30 minutes covered and 30 minutes uncovered.

Apricot Chicken

1 cut up whole Chicken
1 Jar Russian Salad Dressing
½ Jar Apricot Jelly

1 pkg. Dry Onion Soup Mix
Garlic Salt

Mix all ingredients well and pour over chicken. Cover with foil and bake 350 degrees for 1-1½ hours.

Honey-Butter Chicken

1 cut up Chicken
½ lb. melted Butter with ½ to 1 cup Honey to taste.
Sesame Seeds

Melt butter and honey together and drizzle over chicken. Sprinkle with sesame seeds and bake on 350 degrees for 1½ hours, covered.

Brown Rice and Chicken Casserole

2 pkgs. Frozen Broccoli
2 c. cooked Brown Rice
¼ c. chopped Onion
¼ c. chopped Celery
Whole chopped Green Pepper

1 can Cream of Mushroom Soup
1 small can Carnation Milk
1 pkg. Diced Cheddar Cheese
20-10 oz.cans Chicken or
    two cooked Chicken Breasts

Place all mixed ingredients in 9 x 13 casserole and sprinkle cheese on top. Cover and place in 350 degrees oven for 1 hour.

Maple Barbequed Chicken

3 T. Pure Maple Syrup	2 teasp. Dijon Mustard
3 T. Bottled Chili Sauce	4 Skinless Chicken Thighs
1 T. Cider Vinegar	1 T. Vegetable Oil

Stir all ingredients. Oil thighs and pour sauce over them. Bake 350 degrees in oven for 1 hour. Serves 2.

Noodles Florentine

1 (10 oz) pkg. Broad Noodles	1 (12 oz) Frozen Spinach Souffle
1 can Cream of Mushroom Soup	thawed
½ can (soup can) Milk	Bread Crumbs
¾ c. Butter	¼ c. Shredded Cheddar Cheese
¾ c. Shredded Cheddar Cheese	

Cook and drain noodles. Mix soup, milk and ¾ c. cheese and add to noodles. Fold in spinach and pour into 1½ qt. greased casserole. Melt butter and combine with bread crumbs. Mix ¼ cheese with buttered bread crumbs and sprinkle over top of casserole. Bake 350 degrees—1 hour.

Corn Casserole

1 box Jiffy Corn Bread Mix
2 Eggs slightly beaten
1-16 oz. Can Cream Corn
1-16 oz. Can Whole Kernel
   Corn (undrained)

8 oz. Sour Cream
½ c. Butter cut in small pieces
2 qt. Baking dish

Mix all together well. 350 degrees in ungreased baking dish uncovered for 60 minutes or until knife comes out clean from center when testing for doneness.

Layered Vegetable Souffle

2-3 (12 oz.)pkgs. Frozen
   Spinach Souffle
2-3 (12 oz.)pkgs. Frozen
   Corn Souffle

1 (16 oz.) Frozen Sliced
Carrots
2 T. Butter
2 T. Brown Sugar

Layer each vegetable in 9 x 13 baking dish. Dot with butter and brown sugar. Bake uncovered 350 degrees 1 hour.

Sweet Potato Pie

3 or 4 uncooked Yams
½ c. Margarine
2 Eggs

1 c. Sugar
1 teasp. Vanilla

Topping:

½ c. Butter

½ c. Sugar

¼ c. Flour

1 Egg

1-8 oz, can Crushed Pineapple

Bake yams. Mash and peel yams and measure 3 cups yams. Mix with remaining ingredients beating well with mixer. Pour in 8 x 8 baking pan. Prepare topping by creaming butter and sugar and flour. Beat in egg and mix well. Stir in well drained crushed pineapple. Spoon over yams. Bake 350 degrees for 30 minutes.

Buttermilk Kugel

1 lb. Cooked Noodles

4 Eggs

¼ lb. Melted Butter

3 c. Buttermilk

1 T. Sugar

Salt to taste

Add butter to cooked noodles. Add rest of ingredients and mix. Pour in greased 9 x 13 pan bake 375 degrees for 1 hour and 15 minutes.

Another Kugle Version

1 c. Cottage Cheese

1 c. Sour Cream

1-8 oz. Cream Cheese

5 Eggs Beaten

1 Stick melted Butter

½ c. Sugar

1 teasp. Cinnamon

1-16 oz. Pkg. Noodles

2c. Chopped Apples

Mix cheeses, eggs, butter and cinnamon until well blended. Add cooked noodles, apples and optional raisins and mix well. Sprinkle with sugar and cinnamon. Bake in 9 x 13 greased pan of 350 degrees 50-55 minutes.

Pumpkin Mold

1⅔ c. Flour
1⅓ c. Sugar
¼ teasp. Baking Powder
1 teasp. Soda
¾ teasp. Salt

½ teasp. Cinnamon
½ c. Spry
⅓ c. Orange Juice
1 Egg Beaten
1 can Pumpkin

Mix all together and pour into a greased jello mold. Place in 350 degree oven and bake 1 hour uncovered.

Barley Pilaf with Peas

2-10 oz. cans Chicken Broth
½ c. Water
1 c. Quick Pearled Barley
1-10 oz. pkg. Frozen Peas

½ c. chopped Onion
1 Clove Minced Garlic
2 T. Vegetable Oil
2 T. Lite Soy Sauce (optional)

Bring broth to boil with water. Stir in barley. Reduce heat and cover to simmer 10 to 12 minutes or until tender,stirring occasionally. Drain. In large skillet, saute frozen peas, onion and garlic in oil about 5 minutes. Reduce heat and stir in cooked barley and soy sauce. Continue cooking until heated through, stirring occasionally.

Broccoli Salad

3 Large Broccoli Spears,
   flowers only
4 Green Onions
1 c. White or Yellow Raisins

1 c. Mayonnaise
1 c. Spanish Peanuts
3 T. Vinegar or Lemon Juice
2 T. Sugar

Mix all together and refrigerate. Put in peanuts just before serving.

Sounds strange, but it's delicious.

Breads and Muffins

Mom's Famous Bran Muffins

2 c. Nabisco 100% Bran Cereal
1¼ c. Milk
1 c. Flour
⅓ c. Brown Sugar or Honey

2 teasp. Baking Powder
½ teasp, Baking Soda
¼ c. Margarine
1 Egg

Combine all ingredients and mix well. Add ½ to ¾ cup chocolate chips fill greased muffin pan. Bake in a 400 degree oven for 18 minutes.

The chocolate chips make these healthy muffins appealing to kids. It worked for mine.

Batter Herb Bread

½ c. Milk
1½ T. Sugar
1 teasp. Salt
2¼ teasp. Margarine
1 pkg. Yeast

½ c. Warm Water
2¼ c. Flour
1 T. Instant Minced Onion and
Dill

Scald milk and remove from heat. Stir in sugar, butter until dissolved. cool to lukewarm. Dissolve yeast in warm water in a large bowl. Add cooled milk mixture to yeast. Stir flour into mixture and add onions and herbs. Stir until well blended—about 2 minutes. Let rise about 45 minutes. Stir down and beat hard. Turn into greased 8" cake pan or 9" pie pan. Bake in a 350 degree oven for 1 hour. Pour melted butter over bread and sprinkle Kosher salt on top of butter while bread is warm.

Cranberry-Orange Bread

2 c. Flour
1½ teasp. Baking Powder
½ teasp. Baking Soda
1 c. Sugar

2 T. Shortening
1 c. Orange Juice
1 Beaten Egg
1 c. Cranberries

Stir liquid ingredients together. Add dry ingredients. Cut up cranberries into batter. Bake 350 degrees for 50 to 60 minutes in a greased bread loaf pan.

Spiced Pumpkin Bread

3 c. Sugar
1 c. Vegetable oil
3 Large Eggs
1-16 oz. can Pumpkin
3 c. Flour

1 teasp. Ground Cloves
1 teasp. Ground Cinnamon
1 teasp. Ground Nutmeg
1 teasp. Baking Powder
1 c. Chopped Walnuts

Butter and flour 2 bread loaf pans. Beat sugar and oil in large bowl. Mix in eggs and pumpkin. Place all dry ingredients into wet ingredients a little at a time beating with machine after each addition. Mix in walnuts. Bake in 2 pans at 350 degrees about 1 hour 10 minutes. Let cool and remove after checking with knife in the center of bread. Make sure knife comes out clean.

Corn Bread Muffins

2 Eggs
1 c. Sugar
1 c. Oil
1 c. Milk

3 c. Flour
¾ c. Corn Meal
1½ teasp. Baking Powder
1 teasp. Vanilla

Mix all together and bake in muffin pan in a 350 degree oven about 20 minutes. Be sure to grease pan first.

Classic Popovers

2 Large Eggs
¾ c. Milk
¼ c. Water
1 T. Unsalted Butter, Melted

1 c. Minus
2 T. All Purpose Flour
½ teasp. Salt

In bowl, whisk together eggs, milk, and water. Add butter in a stream while whisking batter. Add flour and salt and whisk mixture until combined well but still slightly lumpy. Divide batter among greased six ⅔ c. popover tins. Bake in lower ⅓ of 375 degree oven for 45 minutes. Cut a slit about ½ inch long on top of each popover with a small knife and bake 10 minutes longer.

Chocolate Chip Mondle Bread

½ c. Butter
1 c. Sugar
2 Eggs
1 teasp. Vanilla
1 teasp. Almond Extract
2 c. Flour

1 teasp. Baking Powder
¼ teasp. Cinnamon
½ c. Chocolate Chips
¼ c. Sugar
½ teasp. Cinnamon

Cream butter and sugar. Add eggs, vanilla and almond extract. Stir in flour, baking powder and cinnamon. Add chocolate chips and mix well. With wet hands, divide dough into 2 or 3 parts and make long loaves from each, lying them on greased cookie sheet. Bake 350 degrees for 25 minutes. Remove, slice and sprinkle tops with cinnamon and sugar mixture. Return to oven and bake 5 to 10 minutes longer.

Banana-Chocolate Chip Loaf

3 Ripe Bananas
½ c. Melted Butter
1 c. Sugar
2 Eggs

1 teasp. Vanilla
2 c. Flour
1 teasp. Baking Soda
¾ c. Chocolate Chips

Blend in blender or use mixer for beating wet ingredients. Slowly add dry ingredients and add chocolate chips, mixing by hand. Bake in greased bread loaf for 1 hour in 350 degree oven.

Chocolate Cake

2 c. Flour
1¾ c. Sugar
1 T. Baking Soda
½ c. Cocoa

1 Egg
1 c. Sour Milk
⅔ c. Oil
1 c. Brewed Coffee

Mix all together and bake in a greased 9 x 13 pan on 350 degrees for 30 to 40 minutes.

Bourbon Bread Pudding with Butterscotch Sauce

1 Loaf French Bread	1½ teasp. Vanilla
2 c. Skim Milk	2 Eggs
½ c. Brown Sugar	⅔ c. Raisins
¼ c. Bourbon	Butterscotch Sundae Syrup

Trim crusts from bread and cut in cubes. Arrange single layer on baking sheet and bake until toasted. Combine milk, brown sugar, bourbon, vanilla and eggs and stir well. Add bread crumbs and raisins and toss. Chill 45 minutes. Spoon into 9" square baking dish coated with cooking spray. Cover and bake 350 degrees for 30 minutes, then uncover and bake another 25 minutes or until its set. Serve warm with syrup drizzled over pudding or on the side.

Buster Bar Dessert

1 lb. Oreo Cookies	2 c. Powdered Sugar
½ c. Butter, melted	⅔ c. Chocolate Chips
½ Gallon Vanilla Ice Cream, softened	1½ c. Evaporated Milk
1½ c. Spanish Peanuts	1½ c. Butter
	1 teasp. Vanilla

Crush cookies in food processor or rolling pin. Mix cookie crumbs with ½ c. melted butter and pat in a 9 x 13" pan. Spread ice cream over cookies. Top with peanuts and freeze. Combine powdered sugar, chocolate chips, milk and ½ c. butter. Bring to a boil and simmer 8 minutes, stirring constantly. Remove from heat and add vanilla. Cool and spread over ice cream and nuts. Freeze again until ready to serve.

Brownies

¾ c. Flour	12 ozs. Chocolate Chips
¼ teasp. Baking Soda	1 teasp. Vanilla
¼ teasp. Salt	2 Eggs
⅓ c. Sugar	Powdered Sugar—optional
2 T. Water	

Mix flour, soda and salt together. Cook to boiling the butter, sugar and water stirring constantly. Add 1 c. chocolate chips and vanilla. Stir and transfer to large bowl. Add eggs one at a time beating well after each addition. Gradually blend flour mixture. Stir in chips. Bake in a 9 x 9" greased baking pan. Cool completely. Top with powdered sugar.

Strawberry Pizza

Crust:

1 c. Flour	½ c. Frozen Unsalted Butter
¼ c. Powdered Sugar	

Filling:

1 (8 ozs.) Cream Cheese, softened	½ teasp. Almond Extract
½ c. Sugar	1 qt. Fresh Strawberries
1 teasp. Vanilla	

Glaze:

1 (6 oz.) Jar Red Currant Jelly	2 Whipped Cream
1½ T. Lemon Juice	

Pat crust over 12-13" greased pizza pan and press firmly. Bake 325 degree oven for 15-20 minutes. Cool. Combine cream cheese, vanilla and almond extract and spread over cooked crust. Arrange strawberries on top. Melt jelly, lemon juice by cooking on top of stove in small pan,stirring constantly. Drizzle over fruit and top with whipped cream.

Rice Pudding

2 Large Eggs
½ c. Sugar
2 c. Milk

2 c. Cooked Rice
½ c. Raisins
Little Cinnamon

Mix all together and bake in a 350 degree oven for 1 hour and 15 minutes.

Banana Pudding with Rum

½ c. Plus 2 T. Sugar-divided
¼ c. Flour
2 Eggs separated
1½. Skim Milk

¼ c. Rum
3 Ripe Bananas, sliced
15 Vanilla Wafers

Preheat oven to 425 degrees. In a double broiler place ½ c.sugar and flour. Mix in egg yolks, milk and rum. Cook over high heat stirring constantly until it thickens—about 3 minutes. Reduce heat and cook and stir often 3 more minutes. Spread half on bottom of 9" pie plate and cover with banana slices. Top with wafers. Repeat layers. Beat egg whites and 2 T .sugar. Spoon over and bake about 8 minutes. Refrigerate to chill before serving.

Banana-Caramel Napoleons

1 c. plus 1½ T. Sugar
6 T. Water
1 teasp. Lemon Juice
⅔ c. Whipping Cream
1 Sheet Puff Pastry

12 ozs. Chilled Mascarpone
Cheese
3 Large Bananas
Powered Sugar

Combine 1 c. sugar, 6 T. water and lemon juice in small saucepan. Stir until sugar dissolves. Increase heat and boil. Do not stir until it turns deep amber. Brush down the sides and twirl for 10 minutes. Remove from heat. Carefully add cream and stir until smooth, transfer to bowl. Cover and refrigerate until thick—about 3 hours. Bake puff pastry as directed on package. Cool and slice lengthwise. Fill with caramel filling. Add sliced bananas and cover with top of pastry. Sprinkle powdered sugar before slicing and serve cold. Add chocolate chips, mixing well. Wet hands and divide dough into 3 parts to make loaves. Make 3 separate loafs and lay each on greased cookie sheet, leaving a few inches between each. Bake 350 degrees for 25 minutes. Remove, slice and sprinkle top with cinnamon and sugar mixture. Place back into oven and bake 5 minutes more.

Pumpkin Bars

2 c. Sugar
1 c. Vegetable Oil
1 (15 oz) can Solid Pack
  Pumpkin
2 teasp. Baking powder
1 teasp. Baking soda
½ teasp. Salt
2 teasp. Ground Cinnamon
½ teasp. Ground Ginger
½ teasp. Ground Cloves

½ teasp. Ground Nutmeg
2 c. Flour
6 oz. Cream Cheese at Room
  Temperature
6 T. Butter at Room
  Temperature
1 T. Milk
1 T. Milk
1 teasp. Vanilla
4 c. Powdered Sugar

Preheat oven to 350 degrees. Grease jellyroll sheet. In a mixer, combine sugar and oil. Add eggs and beat well. Beat in pumpkin. Add baking powder, soda and spices. Add flour and blend well. Spread evenly into pan and bake 25 to 30 minutes, until evenly golden, but not dry. Let cool completely. Beat together cream cheese, butter, milk and vanilla. Gradually beat in powdered sugar. Spread frosting over completely cooled bars. Chill or freeze before cutting into bars.

Rum Cake

1 c. Chopped Pecans
1-18 oz. Box Yellow
  Cake Mix
1-3¾ oz. Vanilla Instant
  Pudding
4 Eggs
½ c. Cold Water

½ c. Oil
½ c. Dark Rum (80 proof)
¼ lb. Butter *glaze*
¼ c. Water *glaze*
1 c. Sugar *glaze*
½ c. Rum *glaze*

Preheat oven to 325 degrees. Grease bundt cake pan. Sprinkle nuts
in bottom of pan. Mix all ingredients, other than those that say
glaze next to it, together. Pour into bundt pan and bake 1 hour.
Cool.

Glaze:
Melt butter, stir in water and sugar and boil 5minutes, stirring constantly. Remove from heat and stir in rum. Pour over cake after
removing cake from pan.

Carrot Cake

2½ c. Flour	4 Eggs
2 teasp. Baking Powder	2 c. Grated Carrots
1½ teasp. Baking Soda	1-8 oz. drained, crushed pineapple
3 teasp. Cinnamon	½ c. chopped pecans
2 c. Sugar	½ c. golden raisins
1½ c. Oil	

Sift dry ingredients including cinnamon. In separate bowl beat
sugar, oil and eggs until well blended. Add carrots, pineapple nuts
and raisins. Mix well. Gradually add flour and beat only to combine
well. Bake in greased bundt pan on 350 degrees for 1 hour and
check for doneness.

Cream Cheese Frosting for Carrot Cake

½ c. Butter
1 lb. Powdered Sugar
1 teasp. Vanilla

8 ozs. Cream Cheese
chopped Pecans for top of Icing.

Blend all well and smear on cake. Add pecans over icing.

Sweet Potato Praline Pie

1-16 oz.can of cut Yams
14 ozs. can Sweetened
   Condensed Milk
2 Eggs
1 teasp. Cinnamon

½ teasp. Nutmeg
½ teasp. Ginger
½ c. Chopped Pecans or
   Halved Pecans
9" Pie Shell, unbaked

Topping:
3 T. Dark Brown Sugar
3 T. Whipping cream

Combine ingredients except topping and pecans. Pour into pie shell and bake 50 minutes on 350 degrees. Cool and place pecans over top of pie, combine dark brown sugar and whipping cream and cook slowly, stirring constantly until sugar dissolves. Cook 5 minutes and spoon over pie. Chill in refrigerator and serve with whipped cream if desired.

Apple, Peach or Pear Crisp

4 cups peeled, cored, sliced
   Fresh Fruit (5-7 medium pieces
   of desired fruit)
¾ c. firmly packed Brown Sugar
½ c. Flour

½ c. uncooked Rolled Oats
¾ teasp. Ground Cinnamon
¾ teasp. Ground Nutmeg
⅓ c. Butter, softened

Place sliced fresh fruit in an 8 or 9" baking pan or 1-1½ qt. casserole. Blend remaining ingredients and spread over fruit, bake in a preheated 375 degree oven until fruit is tender and top is brown. About 30 minutes. Serve warm with ice cream if desired.

Tollhouse Fudge

2 T. Butter
1½ c. Sugar
⅔ c. Evaporated Milk
2 c. Mini Marshmallows

1½ c. Chocolate Chips
1 c. Walnuts, chopped
1 teasp. Vanilla

Boil butter, sugar, milk for 5 minutes, stirring constantly. Instantly remove from stove and stir in chocolate chips, marshmallows and vanilla. Place in 8" pan and refrigerate before slicing.

Black Russian Bundt Cake

18 oz.Yellow Cake Mix with Pudding in mix	1 c. Oil
½ c. Sugar	4 Eggs
1-5.9oz. Instant Chocolate Pudding	¼ c. Vodka
	¼ c. Kahlua
	¾ c. Water

Glaze:
½ c. Powdered Sugar
¼ c. Kahlua Liquor

Mix all cake ingredients together and bake in a greased bundt pan in 350 degree oven 60 to 70 minutes. Remove from oven and bundt pan and cool. Mix glaze ingredients in mixer and drizzle over cooled cake.

Special K® Bars

1 c. Sugar	1 c. Peanut Butter
1 c. Light Corn Syrup	6 c. Special K® Cereal
1 6 oz. Chocolate Chips	

Boil sugar and syrup. Blend in peanut butter and Special K® Pour into greased 9 x 13" pan. Top with chocolate chips.

Gingerbread Brownies with Cream Cheese Frosting

1½ c. Flour
1 c. Sugar
¼ c. Unsweetened Cocoa
   Powder
1 teasp. Baking Powder
1 teasp. Ground Ginger
1 teasp. Ground Cinnamon

½ teasp. Baking Soda
½ teasp. Ground Cloves
¼ c. Butter, melted
⅓ c. Molasses
2 Eggs
Cream Cheese Frosting

Combine flour, sugar, cocoa powder, baking powder, ginger, cinnamon, baking soda and cloves in a large mixing bowl. Combine butter, molasses and eggs in another bowl. Add to flour mixture, stirring until combined. Do not beat. The batter will be thick. Spread batter in a greased 13 x 9" baking pan. Bake in a 350 degree oven for 25 minutes. Cool and frost.

Frosting

Beat 2-3oz. packages cream cheese, softened. Add ½ c. butter, softened and 2 teasp. vanilla, beat until light and fluffy. Gradually beat into mixture 2½ to 2¾ c. sifted powdered sugar until frosting is of spreading consistency.

Gingerbread Trifle

1-14 or 14½ oz. package
  Gingerbread mix
⅓ or ½ c. packed
  Brown Sugar.
2 T. Cornstarch
½ teasp. Ground Cinnamon

1½ c. Cherry-cranberry drink
  or Cranberry Juice cocktail
1½ c. frozen pitted tart red cherries
1-29 oz.can Pear Slices, drained
Easy Lemon Cream

Prepare and bake gingerbread mix according to package directions. Cool and cut into 1 inch cubes. For cherry sauce, combine brown sugar (use ½ c. if using cranberry juice cocktail), cornstarch and cinnamon in a medium saucepan. Stir in cherry-cranberry drink, or cranberry juice cocktail. Add frozen cherries. Cook and stir for 2 minutes. Cover and cool without stirring. (sauce can be saved in refrigerator for 3 to 4 days). To assemble,spoon ⅓ of the easy lemon cream into a 3-quart clear glass bowl or souffle dish. Add ⅓ of the cherry sauce. Top with ½ of the gingerbread. Spoon another ⅓ of the lemon cream over gingerbread and continue topping with another ⅓ cherry sauce, (repeat layers).

Easy lemon cream

Beat 1c. whipping cream and 1 teasp. vanilla just until soft peaks form. Fold in 1 c. purchased lemon pudding and stir gently until combined. For creamier texture, stir in 1 T. lemon juice or milk.

Marbled Pumpkin Cake

1 c. Solid Pack Pumpkin
2 teasp. Ground Cinnamon
1 package Yellow Cake mix
4 Eggs

¾ c. Sour Cream
¼ c. Sugar
¼ c. Water
Powdered Sugar, optional

Combine pumpkin and cinnamon in a medium bowl. Combine cake mix, eggs, sour cream, sugar, oil and water in a large mixer bowl. Beat on high speed for 2 minutes. Stir 2½ c. batter into pumpkin mixture. Alternately spoon plain and pumpkin batters into greased 10 c. bundt pan. Bake in preheated 375 degree oven for 40 to 45 minutes or until wooden pick inserted comes out clean. Cool and dust with powdered sugar after removing cake from pan.

Blueberry Crumb Pie

1⅓ c. Flour
½ c. Brown Sugar
½ c. Butter
1½ pints Blueberries

½ c. Sugar
1 teasp. Grated Lemon Rind
½ teasp. Cinnamon
9" Pastry Shell

Mix 1 c. flour and brown sugar. Cut in butter crumbs and set aside for topping. Combine blueberries, sugar, ⅓ c. flour, lemon and cinnamon. Toss, mix well. Spoon into shell. Put on topping. Bake 400 degree oven for 35-40 minutes.

bon appetit !!!!!

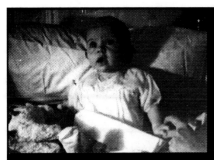

Sandy Kreamer 6 months old

Sisters Bitsy and Sandy

Sandy Kreamer 1 year old

Sandy with outfit her
uncle brought back
from Pacific after
World War II

Sandy Kreamer, 3 years
old, with papa Izadore
Kreamer

Family Rose and Ed
Kreamer, Bitsy sitting,
Sandy standing

Sandy , Stephen and Lisa

Picnic area off highway 100 today—brick stove still stands where pancakes were made—weeds now surround picnic tables.

Farmer's market.

Our first house—1315 Queen Avenue North as it stands today

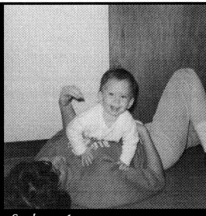

Stephen at 1 year

Stephen at 8 1/2 months

*Stephen at 2 years, in front of
Grandma Rose and Papa's house*

*Stephen's homemade sukkot; 6 years
old*

High School graduation 1982, Eisenhower High School Hopkins, Minnesota

Bar Mitzvah boy's family at Adath Jeshurun Synogogue in Minneapolis, MN.

Graduation with honors, Summa Cum Laude from University of Minnesota

Bar Mitzvah, March 4, 1978; proud grandparents Rose and Ed

Graduation day and out into the real world— Stephen graduated with honors—Cum Laude and Order of the Coif, Northwerstern University Law School, 1990

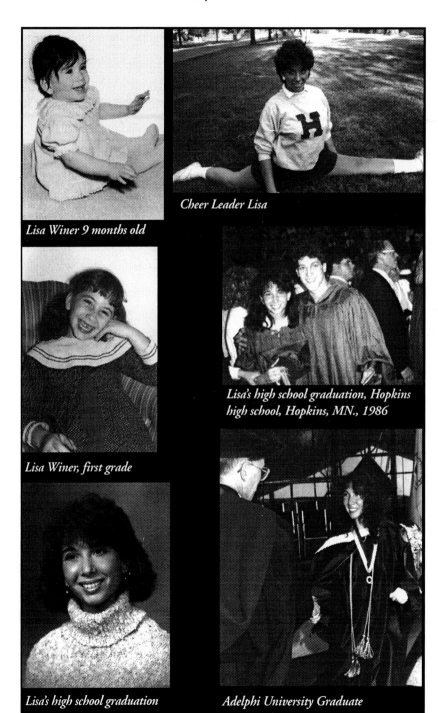

Lisa Winer 9 months old

Cheer Leader Lisa

Lisa Winer, first grade

Lisa's high school graduation, Hopkins
high school, Hopkins, MN., 1986

Lisa's high school graduation

Adelphi University Graduate

Tara, grandma Rose and Bubby
Winer at Mikvah

Baby naming in back yard with Rabbi
Goodman from Adath Jeshurun

TaraLynn's Karate days

Nursery school years

TaraLynn and sister Lisa

Florida, climbing tree
with papa's help

Grown up Tara

Tara met Ed, father, at airport

Tara's first bath in her new home

Adoption, officially ours

Mikvah (Jewish Conversion)

Naturalization and citizenship day

Tara in Duluth 2 years

Julie, Stephen and Sandy Winer, engagement party

Engagement party at Sandy Winer's home, Julie and Stephen

Stephen Winer and Julie Falk, engagement on top of Flat Top Mountain after climbing to the mountain top, September 8, 1996.

Mr. and Mrs. Winer after wedding in Terrytown, New York, June 8, 1997

Outside of the Samuel Clemens home where Stephen and Julie were married with Rachel on right of grandma and papa (Rose and Ed Kreamer)

Bride Lisa

Cutting wedding cake, August 30, 1992

Groom Brett

Stephen and Grandma Rose dancing

Proud grandparents Rose and Ed dancing

At pre nup dinner-Lisa, Tara and Stephen

Pre nup-left to right: Aunt Bitsy, Bride Lisa, Aunt Rachel and Sandy, mother of bride

Flat Top Mt. in Estes Park Colorado; we climbed to the top; Ed, me, Lisa and Stephen

Mom and Tara exploring a cave

South Dakota

Costa Rica—our truck was stuck in the sand; Tara, age 9

Tara with mom and grandma Rose in Colorado

Papa, Stephen, Lisa; Mt. Rushmore South Dakota

Tara fishing in Colorado Rockies

Mountain climbers left to right: Brett Scholder, Stephen and Lisa

Florida—Tara with mom, Grandma Rose, and Papa

Yosemite; Sandy, Stephen and Lisa

Ariah

Morris with Stephen and Lisa

*Deaf kitty Fluffy with broken leg
after falling into wall in new home*

Crazy Fred with Lisa, Stephen and Sandy

*Athena, hit by a car and killed in front
of our house in 1997*

Clive—blond, new cocker Octavia

Camping Days

Left to right: Shirley Cowl, behind her, Hellel Cowl, Mariam Knacht, husband Nate, and Spencers.

Party Gals; Ruth Balto's New Year Party

Sandy, Tara, Stephen, Lisa and Ed

Lisa in play as a Nun during Theatre years—early teens

Ted Balto, Ruth Balto, Aaron Hersch

Stephen, Mom and Tara at Disney World